DATE DUE

DEMCO 38-296

The Marshall Cavendish Illustrated History of

POPULAR MUSIC

Volume 19
1986-1987

MARSHALL CAVENDISH
NEW YORK, LONDON, TORONTO, SYDNEY

Reference Edition Published 1990

ın

ı. Vicenza.

Reference edition produced by DPM Services.

© Orbis Publishing Ltd.MCMLXXXIX
© Marshall Cavendish Ltd.MCMLXXXIX

Set ISBN 1-85436-015-3

Library of Congress Cataloging in Publication Data

The Marshall Cavendish history of popular music.
      p.   cm.
   Includes index.
   ISBN 1-85435-096-X (vol. 17)
   1. Popular music − History and criticism. 2. Rock music − History
and Criticism. I. Marshall Cavendish Corporation. II. Title:
History of popular music.
ML 3470. M36 1988
784.5'009 − dc19   88-21076
                                                       CIP
                                                       MN

Editorial Staff

Editor	Ashley Brown
Executive Editors	Adrian Gilbert Michael Heatley
Consultant Editors	Richard Williams Peter Brookesmith
Editorial Director	Brian Innes

Reference Edition Staff

Reference Editor	Mark Dartford
Revision Editor	Fran Jones
Consultant Editor	Michael Heatley
Art Editor	Graham Beehag

CONTENTS

CONTRIBUTORS

CLIVE ANDERSON

Co-author of *The Soul Book* and contributor to *Encyclopedia of Rock*, he has also written for *Black Music, Black Echoes, New Kommotion* and other magazines.

STEPHEN BARNARD

Has contributed to *Atlantic Rock, Melody Maker* and the *Rock Files* series. He also lectures at the City University, London.

DICK BRADLEY

Completed his PhD thesis on *British Popular Music in the Fifties* at the Centre of Contemporary Cultural Studies in Birmingham, England, and has also written articles for *Media, Culture & Society.*

JOHN BROVEN

Author of *Walking to New Orleans* and *South of Louisiana,* he has also contributed to *Nothing but the Blues* and *Encyclopedia of Rock.* He writes for *Blues Unlimited* and has also compiled several New Orleans rhythm and blues anthologies

ROB FINNIS

Author of *The Phil Spector Story* and *The Gene Vincent Story,* he has contributed to the major rock journals and runs a specialist record shop.

SIMON FRITH

A lecturer at the University of Warwick, England, he has built up a reputation over the last 15 years as one of the leading international commentators on rock music. He has co-edited the *Rock File* series, and written *The Sociology of Rock.*

PETER GURALNIK

Author of *Feel Like Going Home, Lost Highway* and *Nighthawk Blues,* his articles on blues, country and rock have appeared in *Rolling Stone,* the *Village Voice, Country Music, Living Blues,* the *New York Times* and the *Boston Phoenix.*

BILL HARRY

Founder member of UK's *Mersey Beat,* he later became news editor of *Record Mirror* and music columnist for *Weekend.* He is currently an independent PR for such artists as Suzi Quatro and Kim Wilde.

MARTIN HAWKINS

An acknowledged expert on the Sun era of rock'n'roll (author of *The Sun Story*), he writes for *Melody Maker, Time Barrier Express* and *Country Music*

BRIAN HOGG

Publisher of *Bam Balam,* which concentrates on US and UK bands of the Sixties, he has also written for such magazines as *New York Rocker* and *Record Collector.*

PETER JONES

Was editor of UK's *Record Mirror* from 1961 to 1969. He then became UK News editor of *Billboard* in 1977 and later UK and European Editor.

ROBIN KATZ

After 10 years in the Motown Press Office, she now writes freelance for *New Sound, New Styles, International Musician* and *Smash Hits.*

JOE McEWEN

An acknowledged authority on soul music, he has written for *Rolling Stone, Phonograph Record, Black Music,* the *Boston Phoenix* and Boston's *Real Paper.*

BILL MILLAR

As a freelance journalist he writes for *Melody Maker* and other rock papers. He is the author of *The Drifters* and *The Coasters.*

DAVID MORSE

Author of *Motown,* he lectures at the School of English and American Studies at Sussex University, England.

TONY RUSSELL

Editor of *Old Time Music* from 1971, he contributes regularly to *Blues Unlimited* and *Jazz Journal* and is the author of *Blacks, Whites and Blues.*

ROBERT SHELTON

Has written about blues, country and folk for the *New York Times,* London *Times, Listener, Time Out* and *Melody Maker.*

NICK TOSCHES

Author of *Hellfire,* a biography of Jerry Lee Lewis, he also writes for *New York Times* and *Village Voice.*

MICHAEL WATTS

Writes on popular arts for *The Los Angeles Times* and London *Times* and is rock columnist for *Records and Recording Magazine.*

ADAM WHITE

Has written about Motown for *Music Week* and *Black Echoes,* and scripted a six-hour documentary about the company and its music for US radio. Also worked as managing editor of *Billboard* magazine in New York.

Soul Spectrum

The Eighties soul scene – a dazzling kaleidoscope of colours, sounds and styles

THE HISTORY OF SOUL music over the years reveals a picture rich in both diversity and tradition. The Eighties brought several innovations in the field of black music – particularly with the growing popularity of electro-funk – but styles of old remained, as evidenced by the continuing importance of Motown.

Although the label had long since lost its standing as 'The Sound of Young America', it continued to exert an influence both inside and outside the soul field by virtue of its back catalogue, promoted vigorously by the company's publishing arm, Jobete Music, providing Eighties hits for Phil Collins, Leo Sayer and others, and heavily influencing white pop groups like Culture Club.

Scratching the surface

Jazz-funk, an offshoot of disco in which the virtuosity of the performers was often as prized as their image and material, came to popularity in the late-Seventies UK club scene. Meanwhile, in America, ideas first apparent in Seventies Eurodisco came to their logical conclusion in the field of electro-funk. Synthesisers squealed, rhythm boxes pounded the beat and melody was at a premium – this was almost a form of soul-less soul for the dance floor.

Non-musicians began to get in on the act, making music through 'scratching', the DJ-inspired craze of rhythmically manipulating discs on the turntable, and 'rapping', the talkover technique borrowed from reggae toasters

The success of Michael Jackson (below) with his Thriller *album of 1982 seemed likely to prove a hard act for others to follow. The record provided a clutch of transatlantic hit singles, while Jackson reversed the trend towards faceless, mechanistic dance-floor funk by backing each single release with an inventive promotional video.*

that threatened to become the Eighties equivalent of doowop. If the spotlight had shifted from the concert stage to the disco in the Seventies, the spontaneity of these innovations made the disco console the Eighties soul stage.

In commercial terms, the success story of the early Eighties was that of former Motown artist Michael Jackson. He followed up *Off The Wall*, his disco-oriented chart-topper of 1979, with the blockbusting *Thriller* (1982), which sold over 10 million copies worldwide and provided innumerable hit singles. The record merged elements of Motown soul, disco and even heavy rock; guitarist Eddie Van Halen's lead break in 'Beat It' single-handedly started a craze for a rock-soul synthesis.

Yet despite the growing claims of technology and the eclipse of the soul vocal stylist, there were still familiar sounds to be heard. The swooping string arrangements of the late lamented Philadelphia International label lived on in the work of the Chic Organization, while the Earth Wind and Fire horn section added spice to numerous releases in a manner reminiscent of the Memphis Horns some 15 years previously. It could safely be assumed that soul music would continue to draw inspiration from a wide variety of sources and recycle them into many familiar—yet intriguingly different—forms.

MICHAEL HEATLEY

EARTH WIND & FIRE

A band with all the elements of success

EARTH WIND AND FIRE were essentially the creation of Maurice White, an unlikely visionary born in Memphis, Tennessee, on 19 December 1944. At the age of six, he was already singing with a gospel quartet at Rose Hill Baptist Church. By the age of 12, he had decided to concentrate on drumming and accordingly threw himself into numerous school talent shows, at which fellow strivers included Booker T. Jones, Isaac Hayes and David Porter.

These halcyon days in Memphis ended in 1960 when he was taken from under the wing of an indulgent grandmother and spirited off to join his parents in Chicago. Father had qualified as a physician and Maurice, it was deemed, should follow his example. He dutifully enrolled at Roosevelt University but soon switched to the Chicago Music Conservatory. By 1963 he was working four nights a week at the Hungry I Club and doing session work for Chess Records during the daytime. At Chess he learned the niceties of drumming along with discipline, teamwork, commercial sense, composing and production skills and played behind an incredible array of artists including Muddy Waters, Howlin'

Wolf, Buddy Guy, Koko Taylor, Etta James, Fontella Bass, Billy Stewart, Sonny Stitt and Ramsey Lewis, who asked White to join his trio.

Elemental energy

Lewis was a no-nonsense piano player with the sounds of the church in his bones and a sharp ear for the kind of funk the customers wanted. Maurice, together with bassist Cleveland Eaton, replaced Red Holt and Eldee Young in the Ramsey Lewis Trio where they stayed from 1965 to 1970, laying down 10 albums and scoring pop hits with 'Wade In The Water' (1966) and others. When Maurice quit it was to form the Salty Peppers (together with Don Barry, Louis Satterfield and Don Whitehead) who enjoyed some success in Chicago, where they played the clubs and lent their talents to TV commercials.

Later in 1970, the Salty Peppers folded and White began to formulate Earth Wind and Fire, a name that hinted at his interest in astrology. The group's original line-up consisted of Maurice, his brother Verdine (bass), Michael Beale (guitar, harmonica), Wade Flemmons (vocals), Yackov Ben Israel (percussion, congas), Sherry Scott (vocals), Alex Thomas (trombone), Chet Washington (tenor sax) and Don Whitehead (keyboards). The band signed to Warner Brothers and began to record in Los Angeles.

From the outset, Earth Wind and Fire were not a traditional soul band. Apart from a tenuous connection with jazz, courtesy of Maurice, their antecedents were in the good-time traditions of R&B. The white feedback into black music had resulted in the fusion music of outfits like the Chambers Brothers, Fifth Dimension, Santana, Chicago, Tower of Power, Graham Central Station, the Ohio Players, Rare Earth and LaBelle, modified over the decade by a kaleidoscope of contributions from Miles Davis, Weather Report, Milton Nascimento and Stevie Wonder. It was here, amid memories of 'flower power' and Aquarian dreams, that the roots of Earth Wind and Fire lay.

Fan the Fire
Earth Wind And Fire, their first LP, was produced by Joe Wissert and emerged in 1971. Most of the songs were written by Maurice White, Flemmons and Whitehead and ranged through hard funk, apocalyptic gospel, latin and jazz to mainstream R&B. 'Fan The Fire', a single released in April, had served as a taster for the album, but more indicative of things to come was 'Love Is Life', released with the album, which coupled R&B with mystical pronouncements on the nature of the universe.

Their second LP – *The Need Of Love*, issued in December 1971 – was undeniably potent and more than a trifle odd. Sub-Hendrix rock, lyrical love ballads and greasy R&B filled side one, while the schizophrenic nature of the band was signalled on side two by an extended jam called 'Energy'. Beginning with a murderous assault on the drum kit, it flirted with the memory of John Coltrane before devolving into doggerel on the mystery of existence.

Hardly surprisingly, these first two albums failed to ignite public interest; in an era of classic soul, when every other artist seemed torn from the bosom of the church, down on one knee sweating and testifying, Earth Wind and Fire seemed dangerously cerebral. Indeed in some quarters they were even construed as dangerously white – campus clowns with jazz affiliations and no campus!

The group now left Warners, recorded a one-off soundtrack album for Stax and

Opposite: The massed horns, percussion section and instrumentalists of Earth Wind and Fire. Above: Maurice White selects some EW&F favourites on the juke-box.

signed a new deal with Columbia. The first album for the new label, *Last Days And Time*, released in January 1972, saw a new line up: Maurice and Verdine were joined by Philip Bailey (vocals, congas, percussion), Larry Dunn (keyboards, clarinet), Ralph Johnson (drums, percussion), Ronnie Laws (reeds), Roland Bautista (guitar) and Jessica Cleaves (vocals). Production remained in the hands of Joe Wissert both for this set and its June 1973 follow-up, *Head To The Sky*, on which Bautista and Laws were replaced by Al McKay and Andrew Woodfolk respectively, while an extra member was recruited in guitarist Johnny Graham.

The cover artwork of *Head To The Sky* mirrored White's spiritual pretensions: Jessica, in white turban and sexy kaftan, was surrounded by bare-chested males in the last stages of lotus-posture boredom as flowers exploded outward and a bearded Maurice presided benignly over proceedings. The album's lyrics were equally embarrassing but the music itself was superb, a winning blend of Forties scat, Chicano shuffle, West Coast whimsy and unbrindled exotica, densely percussive and layered in construction.

All the faults and virtues that made Earth Wind and Fire such maddening, intoxicating entertainers were well established by the time they unveiled *Open Our Eyes* in April 1974. The album track 'Kalimba Story' was the White brothers' declaration of intent to make 'future music' and the track 'Mighty Mighty', which was released as a single and made Number 29 in the US charts, proved a success. In October, 'Devotion' gave the group another hit and mass acceptance seemed to be just around the corner. It came with a soundtrack album, *That's The Way Of The World*, in March: polished, tight harmonies, alto voices led by Bailey congregating over busy rhythms and thrusting brass – all characterised this set and carried the single 'Shining Star' to Number 1 in the same month.

On the next album, *Gratitude* (1975), the

group's drum sound was boosted by the addition of Fred White while another newcomer, Don Myrick, contributed eloquent sax. The LP marked time with useful live renditions of their best-known numbers and provided a souvenir of the band's staggering stage show, which featured, among many treats, lasers, levitating drummers and vanishing acts.

Spirits in wonderland
The following year, Maurice White and arranger/producer Charles Stepney, whom White had first met back in his Chess days, produced another studio album. Dedicated to Stepney, who died during the sessions, *Spirit* represented a further polishing of that supreme style – all sound and fury, perhaps signifying nothing – that defined the group. The title track served up the usual sentimental nonsense – 'everytime you smile, you bless a child' – but generally the album felt fine and 'Saturday Nite', with its blazing horn riff, provided another US hit single at Number 21.

In December 1977, *All'n'All* was released; the new LP revealed Maurice White up to his neck in ill-conceived metaphysics – but behind the obsession with Egyptology, pyramid power and arcane matters dear to Californians surged a remarkable sound. Judged on these grounds, as pure sound only, 'Serpentine Fire' and 'Fantasy' were brilliantly executed pieces and kept the group in the singles charts. *The Best Of Earth Wind And Fire Volume 1*, released in December 1978, supplied only three new songs but the choppily percussive 'Love Music', an irresistible 'September' and a blistering big-band version of Lennon-McCartney's 'Got To Get You Into My Life', recorded for the *Sgt Pepper's Lonely Hearts Club Band* film of 1978, fully confirmed the group's supremacy.

The Earth Wind and Fire production line rolled on with *I Am* in June 1979, and although critical plaudits were restrained it still yielded two sizeable hits. The first, 'Boogie Wonderland', featured female vocal group the Emotions in full cry and was aimed unashamedly at the nation's feet, while the second – 'After The Love Has Gone' – was a devastating ballad, gently gilded by Don Myrick's smooth tenor sax and equal to anything ventured by the newly-romantic Commodores. These followed 'September' and 'Life' into the US Top Ten, while marking the group's greatest level of success in the UK, where they notched up three Top Five singles in just over half a year. New writers like Brenda Russell were employed for the next LP, an adventurous double set entitled *Faces* (1980), but despite superb singles in 'Let Me Talk', 'Pride' and 'Faces', sales were disappointing.

The streamlined *Raise* fared better on release in November 1981. Eschewing mysticism and again favouring outside writers, it had a sharpness appropriate to the time. The bright-eyed 'Let's Groove' made Number 3 in the US as a single, while those who graduated to the album were rewarded with slinky delights like 'My Love'.

Back to earth

The group appeared to be on an even keel once more, although their huge, racially mixed audiences in America and the UK were now being seduced by the snappy sounds of Shalamar and other stylish funk outfits, while various members of Earth Wind and Fire were increasingly sidetracked into production and session work.

Maurice had long been successfully involved with Ramsey Lewis, Deniece Williams and the Emotions, and by 1983 had turned his attention to Jennifer Holiday. Having flexed his muscles with Pockets, Verdine finally settled for producing Britain's Level 42 with the assistance of Larry Dunn. The latter had completed

Maurice White, undisputed leader of Earth Wind and Fire, plays his kalimba (below) and fronts his all-singing, all-dancing band on stage (far right and below right) as brother Verdine levitates (right).

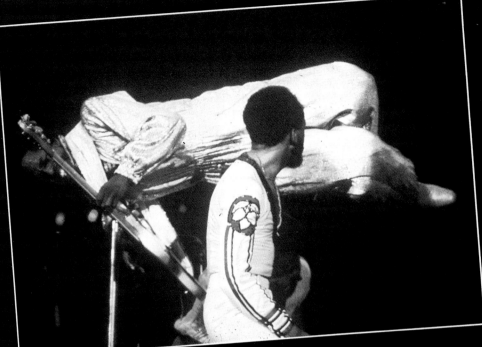

projects with Stanley Turrentine, Caldera and Lenny White, while Al McKay swung into action with Ren Woods, the Mighty Clouds of Joy and Finis Henderson. In August 1983, under the aegis of George Duke, lead singer Philip Bailey stepped out with his own album *Continuation*.

1983's *Powerlight* made Number 12 in the US, but the following year's *Electric Universe* barely scraped into the Top Forty. It was deemed time for solo projects, and Richard Bailey took off in 1985 with *Chinese Wall* and its Number 1 UK/Number 2 US single 'Easy Lover'. But further success was harder to come by and 1987 saw EW&F return with *Touch The World*.   CLIVE ANDERSON

Earth Wind and Fire
Recommended Listening

The Best Of Earth Wind And Fire Vol 1 (CBS 83284) (Includes: Fantasy, Shining Star, Got To Get You Into My Life, September, Reasons, Singasong); *I Am* (CBS 86084) (Includes: Boogie Wonderland, Let Your Feelings Show, In The Stone, Can't Let Go, You And I, Star).

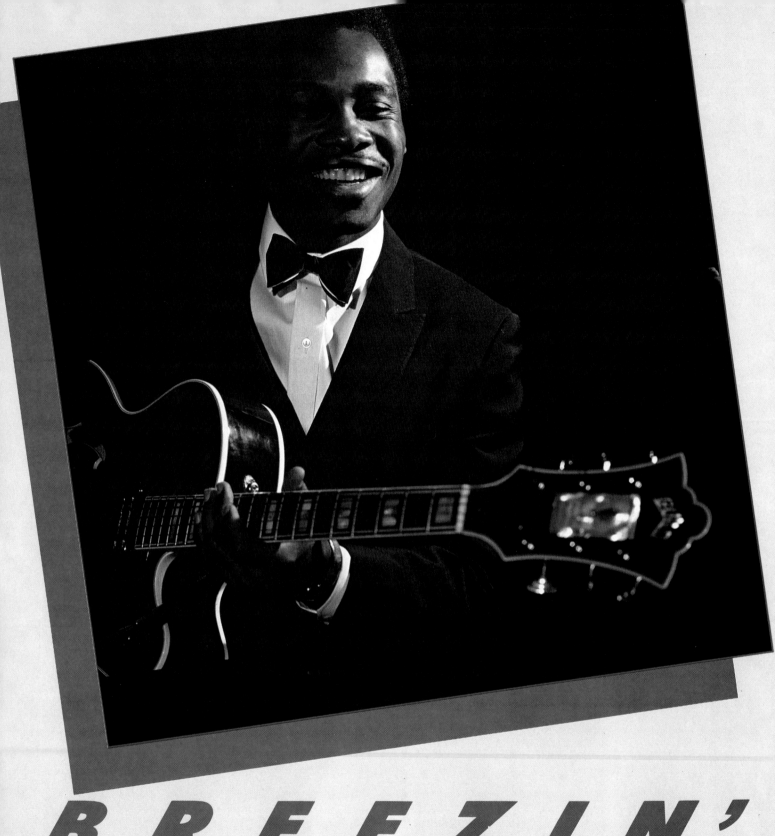

BREEZIN'

The cool night airs of George Benson

IN THE HERE-TODAY, gone-tomorrow world of rock music, George Benson is a scarce commodity indeed: a technically brilliant master of his instrument, a fine vocalist and a giant of two very different spheres of music – modern jazz and soul/disco.

It is this last quality above all that sets George Benson apart from his other gifted contemporaries. Virtually single-handedly, and in less than half-a-dozen albums, he crossed the once incompatible boundaries of mainstream instrumental jazz and classy pop, introducing audiences to a new brand of music in the process.

Benson was born in the mid Forties (his exact birthdate seems to be a well-kept secret) into a strictly religious, poor family in Pittsburgh, Pennsylvania. His step-father, a keen admirer of jazz guitarist Charlie Christian, made George his first makeshift guitar from empty cigar boxes and, at the age of four, George entered and won a local amateur singing contest. After graduating to ukelele and, at the age of eight, getting his first real acoustic guitar, Master Benson spent leisurely evenings and weekends supplementing his pocket money by busking. Two years later, he was spotted by a talent scout from RCA and signed to their X label, a black subsidiary, for which he later cut a couple of instrumental singles.

Heavily influenced by virtuoso guitarist Wes Montgomery, later a close friend and mentor, the teenage Benson took up the electric guitar, serving his apprenticeship in local jazz clubs. His other notable influences included Hank Garland, Grant Green and his stepfather's favourite, Charlie Christian. At the age of 18, Benson first heard the music of saxophonist Charlie Parker and his love for jazz became all-consuming.

Meet the new boss

He joined Brother Jack McDuff's Organ Trio in the early Sixties, gaining valuable experience from the group's almost constant schedule of one-nighters across the United States; then in 1964, after recording an album with McDuff for the Prestige label entitled *New Boss Guitar Of George Benson With The Brother Jack McDuff Quartet*, Benson left to form his own jazz-oriented group. A succession of jazz albums for different labels followed, two each on Columbia and Verve and three for A&M, before Benson settled in under experienced producer Creed Taylor at CTI in 1971. A good example of Benson's Sixties work is *The Other Side Of Abbey Road* (1969), an interesting, but largely uninspired re-working of the Beatles' album.

Over the next five years at CTI, Benson fulfilled his considerable promise as a guitarist, recording six albums – notably *White Rabbit* (1972) and *Bad Benson* (1974) – and building a strong and respected following in jazz circles. At the same time, however, he was becoming aware of jazz music's biggest problems: it had little commercial appeal and catered mainly to a sophisticated cult audience. A 1975 single, 'Supership', made Number 30 in the UK, but Benson remained largely unknown to mass audiences.

This state of affairs changed dramatically the following year when Benson left CTI and joined Warner Brothers. There, under the wing of Bob Krasnow, he was teamed with ace producer Tommy LiPuma and recorded the album *Breezin'* (1976). Although five of the six cuts were instrumentals, LiPuma gave Benson the freedom to show off his unique vocal style on a smoochy half-jazz, half-soul version of Leon Russell's 'This Masquerade', written in 1972. Benson had occasionally sung on record before, but his vocals had nearly always featured well down in the mix. On 'This Masquerade' LiPuma brought out Benson's rich, baritone voice to act as a silky smooth counterpoint to the track's expertly woven guitar passages.

Released as a single, 'This Masquerade' made Number 10 on the *Billboard* Hot Hundred and became the first record to top both the US jazz and soul charts simultaneously. *Breezin'* went platinum and later became the biggest-selling jazz album of all time, garnering Benson countless awards that included three Grammys.

Opposite: George Benson – the acceptable face of soul? Above: The guitarist finds a vocal partner in Aretha Franklin.

Having finally found the magic hit formula Benson, again with LiPuma at the helm, recorded *In Flight* (1977), a million-selling follow-up which, now aimed at a different audience, comprised four vocal tracks and only two instrumentals. Without doubt the album's highlight was an exquisitely sung version of 'Nature Boy', Nat 'King' Cole's 1948 hit written by eden ahbez, a Brooklyn-born yogi who believed that only divinities were worthy of capital initials for their names.

Into orbit

The success of *In Flight* brought Benson superstar status, with world tours, guest appearances on recordings by artists ranging from Herbie Hancock to Minnie Riperton, innumerable awards (including several more Grammys), an invitation to record the soundtrack for the Muhammad Ali movie *The Greatest* (1977), wardrobe credits on his album sleeves, and lilting duets – on which the voracious US record industry seems to thrive – with Aretha Franklin, Chaka Khan and Patti Austin. Superstardom for Benson also meant the opportunity to fulfil every guitarist's dream: to be given a free hand to design his own guitars, custom-made for him by Ibanez. His small-bodied, semi-acoustic GB10 became a familiar Benson trademark.

After *In Flight* and, in particular, the brilliant double album, *Livin' Inside Your Love* (1979), Benson's recordings leaned increasingly toward pop/soul to the almost total exclusion of jazz; it could be argued that he had once again become stuck in an artistic rut just as he was in his pre-*Breezin'* days – albeit this time a highly profitable and commercially successful one. Most of the numbers George Benson recorded were well-chosen standards or specially-commissioned material.

In 1980 Quincy Jones, fresh from his staggering success with Michael Jackson's *Off The Wall* (1979), produced the biggest-selling Benson album to date, the late-night listening, disco-inspired *Give Me The Night*, which yielded two smash hit singles in the title track and 'Love X Love'. The 1981 Benson anthology *The George Benson Collection* featured, in best record industry tradition, two all-new compositions, 'Turn Your Love Around' and 'Never Give Up On A Good Thing', both very danceable and both produced by Jay Graydon. Benson's 1983 offering, *In Your Eyes*, was produced by Turkish-born Arif Mardin, formerly the Atlantic label's disco mastermind, with a little help from Kashif. Early 1985 saw the release of his album *20/20*.

Benson's popularity with the Eighties record-buying public is undoubted, and he has also exerted a considerable influence on new musicians. UK band Central Line, for example, scored a hit in early 1983 with 'Nature Boy' inspired, they openly admit, purely by Benson's 1977 version. In fact it is debatable whether they had even heard the original recording. Benson's success in crossing over from mainstream jazz to mainstream pop also opened the doors for a new wave of jazz-funk musicians, typified by such artists as Grover Washington Jr in the US and Iceland's Mezzoforte.

Benson's superb, instinctive jazz feel reflected not only in his inimitable guitar work but also, since 1976, in his soulful vocals, sets him apart from other black singers, disco exponents and jazz masters and will ensure him a lasting place in the history of rock.

MARK LEWISOHN

CYBERNETIC SOUL

THE STORY OF black music in the early Eighties can be told through three related images: the street, the studio and outer space. These images have rebounded around the galaxy of popular music, creating new styles of dance, new attitudes to musical production and a new generation of performers. Slumped against a decaying wall in the South Bronx is the solid frame of Afrika Bambaataa; beside him on a square of cardboard a B. Boy shudders stiffly like a robot coming to life, and the perfect beat of an Arthur Baker mega-mix escapes from the high-tech chrome of a portable stereo cabinet.

Bambaataa embodies the new era. Leader of one-time street gang the Black Spades, since magically transformed into a cultural army called the Zulu Nation, he has the respect of break dancers, rappers and graffiti artists throughout the universe of hip-hop style. At the turntables

Was this the final frontier of dance music?

of New York's Roxy Club, where the floor erupts with electro body dancers, or in the studios of the independent Tommy Boy label, where he guides the techno tracks of his group, the Soul Sonic Force, Afrika Bambaataa patrols the planets of a new musical style.

The hard dance beat of Black American funk meets the synthetic sound of European pop, as bodies pop and B. Girls freeze-frame across the floor. A rough mix of Spyder D's 'Smerphies Dance' raps and crackles through gigantic speakers as an electric current shoots through the night. This is music moving to the next phase – new technology and versions of a future galaxy stolen by the street crews in their search for the sharpest dance style.

Human bodies, moving like androids, crank to the beat of black music in orbit. The Eighties is the dawning of a new dance stance: the era of 'cybernetic soul'.

Sidewalk invaders

Friday night at Manhattan's Funhouse in the early Eighties was a ritual celebration of cybernetic soul. Dance crews from the boroughs converged on the club, bearing their allegiances on shortened T-shirts – 'East Side Electric Force', 'The Sidewalk Invaders', 'Shock Squad'. The music they carried with them in portable blasters and in the data banks of their new-world minds blended all categories of pop. The punk-funk of Prince's '1999' dressed funk in the aggressive style of European new wave, the funk'n'roll of Rick James' 'Cold Blooded' added rock licks to the hard edges of urban soul, while the white synth-pop of Britain's Thomas Dolby and the Human

League also found space in the Funhouse. A gigantic clown's head housed the DJ's console — inside was one of the city's sharpest pulses, John 'Jellybean' Benitez, master of a million remixes.

Benitez was just one of a new generation of producers of which Arthur Baker and John Robie, who mixed hits for Rockers' Revenge, Planet Patrol and New Order, were the best known, followed by Raul Rodriguez, one-time DJ at New York New York, who produced two Funhouse anthems: Man Parrish's 'Hip Hop Be Bop (Don't Stop)' and Two Sisters' 'High Noon'. Those extended 12-inch dance tracks, waxed in the heat of the disco inferno, once threatened to diminish the role of the DJ, but actually achieved the opposite.

Larry Levan, DJ at Manhattan's Paradise Garage, made the meteoric journey from programmer to producer and finally to performer as a member of the New York City Peech Boys, whose 'Don't Make Me Wait' was a devastating example of the new sound. Mixing was the discipline of cybernetic soul; each new production brought with it a battery of possibilities: the club mix, the dub mix, the acappella version, the atomic shot, the mega-mix and of course the scratch mix. In the words that were immortalised by the soothing DJ of Indeep's 'Last Night A DJ Saved My Life', the mix actually had the power to heal: 'There's not a problem that I can't fix/I can do it in the mix.'

Digital dancing

Cybernetic soul did not emerge out of the clubs alone; it developed alongside a new group of independent labels, including Tommy Boy, Streetwise and Profile, and seized the power of new technology. The Sony Walkman personal stereo introduced the term 'wired for soul', while the portable stereo, known variously as a 'ghetto blaster', 'vox box' or 'Third World briefcase', turned urban streets, subways and the parks into dub clubs. Inside the recording studios themselves, new digital facilities, new computer banks and advanced synthesisers gave rise to a high-tech musical culture. The term 'electro-funk' controversially edged its way into the history of black music.

George Clinton, a musical innovator with Parliament, Funkadelic and others, was at the forefront of the major developments in the universe of cybernetic soul. His album *Computer Games* (1983), a bizarre journey into the infotech world of computers, synth drums, tape loops, vocoders and Lyricon synthesisers, seemed likely to become one of the classic albums of the early Eighties while the single, 'Loopzilla', saw a tape loop of just eight seconds of recorded music sculptured into a monumental dance-track that included snatches from 15 years of music. Old Motown met new funk in a cybernetic style as the microchip, the machine and the human mind created the music for digital dancers to move to.

In the summer of 1983, the Washington-

Opposite: Afrika Bambaataa leads the Soul Sonic Force. Inset above: Rock meets soul in the music of Rick James. Above: Electro body dancing at the Roxy Club, New York.

based independent label DETT released a cybernetic club mix called 'Search And Destroy', which merged the hard-edged percussion of funk with a barrage of space-age effects drawn from computer technology and science fiction. The name of the record was taken from a video game, and the name of the group – Arcade Funk – was an open admission that computer games and space invader machines were shaping the expectations of a new generation of record buyers.

Space: the final frontier

The robotic rhythm of electrofunk was produced by deliberately anonymous groups, often consisting of studio producers, whose names read like a litany of extra-terrestrial culture. New names appeared almost every week – the Packman, Cybotron, G. Force, Orbit – and even the pages of *Billboard* had to take account

of the electro revolution.

New music invariably challenges established attitudes, and electro-funk caused more controversy than any other development in black music with its heavy emphasis on synthesised instrumentals which tended to push vocals to the periphery. Electrofunk became the style of the B. Boys but the enemy of R&B purists. For some people, it simply had no relationship to soul and no place in the history of black music – but for others it was a form of new romantic pop with a gloss of funk and seemed to point to a rich future.

The term cybernetic soul means something more than electro-funk: it implies a meeting of humans and machines and the coming together of tradition and innovation. The voice of soul enriches the tempo set by the new machines. In 1982 a Boston group once known as the Energetics were transformed by Tommy Boy records from a vocal quintet into a unit known as Planet Patrol. The line that runs from the Dramatics to *Star Wars*' Darth Vader had been drawn. Cybernetic soul: where the robots meet their roots.   STUART COSGROVE

One Nation Under A Groove

Flying the funk flag with George Clinton

GEORGE CLINTON is soul music's most irrepressible fantasy. Dressed in a flamboyant wig, silver high-heeled boots, a pair of red nylon tights and a cape that shimmers with the excessive glitter of high camp, he inhabits an eccentric universe. Starships from outer space, strip-cartoon characters, monsters and Martians are thrown together into a bizarre science-fiction comedy. This is black music in the world of parody. Batman and Robin, the Lone Ranger and Tonto and the fearless exploits of Flash Gordon are forgotten when Clinton and his assistant William 'Bootsy' Collins cruise the galaxies to recycle funk through fantasy and fiction.

Standing for Parliament

Born in Blainfield, Ohio, Clinton became lead singer with doowop group the Parliaments during the Fifties and recorded a couple of singles – 'Poor Willie' (for ABC in 1956) and 'Lonely Island' (for New Records in 1958) – before signing to Motown. None of the Parliaments' recordings for this label were ever released, however, and it was not until 1967 when the group cut a single for Revilot Records, that they first tasted success. '(I Wanna) Testify' reached Number 20 in the US charts and 'All Your Goodies Are Gone' gave them another, albeit minor, hit later the same year.

Clinton was also employed by Revilot as a staff songwriter and was responsible for numerous dance tracks, including Darrell Banks' go-go classic 'Our Love (Is In The Pocket)'. Somewhere along the way the Parliaments lost their mohair suits and the last letter of their name and were transformed into Parliament, the first family of eccentric funk. Disillusioned with the restrictiveness of mainstream soul and the tiresome way in which vocal groups had institutionalised a slick uniform of matching shirts and formation dancing, Clinton broke loose. The Seventies became his decade of new extravagance – the period of P. Funk.

Parliament became the meeting-place for two powerful traditions in the field of soul. Clinton introduced the vocal harmonies of his own past and strengthened the fabric of his new sound with musicians drawn from the JBs, those hard-edged rhythm masters who had been the backbone of James Brown's pioneering street funk. Parliament had the baddest and the best: the brass constructions of Fred Wesley, the piercing saxophone of Maceo Parker and the basslines of Bootsy

Opposite: Parliament broke free of all restriction to create their own wild funk style. Top right: On stage with a cast of thousands. Right: George Clinton, Parliament's inimitable lead singer.

traced in his influence rather than in hit records. Although most critics see the international success of Funkadelic's 'One Nation Under A Groove – Part 1', which reached Number 28 in the US charts and Number 9 in the UK in 1978, as Clinton's greatest moment, his music has paved the way for a number of massively important developments. The collusion of punk and funk in recordings like Prince's 'Ronnie Talk To Russia', the funk'n'roll style of Rick James and Nona Hendryx's transformation from LaBelle to B.Girl could not have happened without George Clinton's pioneering work.

Down-to-earth
In 1975, Casablanca Records released Clinton's definitive album, Parliament's *Mothership Connection*, which was a space-age fantasy steeped in the new style of cybernetic soul. The album told the story of an extra-terrestrial invasion in which strange beings invade the earth bringing with them the music of the mothership: 'Good Evening. Do not attempt to adjust your radio. We have taken control to bring you this special show. We will return it to you as soon as you are groovy. Welcome to Station WEFUNK, better known as WeFunk or deeper still the Mothership Connection, home of the extra-terrestrial brothers, dealers of funky music: P.Funk, uncut funk, the bomb . . .'

'Give Up The Funk (Tear The Roof Off The Sucker)', a mid-Seventies celebration of dance, excess and the shock of the new, was lifted from the LP to reach Number 15 in the US singles charts. Along with Marvin Gaye's *What's Going On* (1971) and Stevie Wonder's *Innervisions* (1972), *Mothership Connection* deserves its reputation as one of the most influential albums to come out of America in the Seventies.

In 1983, when George Clinton arrived in Britain to promote *Computer Games*, his first ever solo album after more than 20 years of recording, he brought with him a timely reminder of the style and wit of ghetto eccentricity. He appeared on television to present a live version of his funk single 'Loopzilla', and visibly shocked an audience weaned on new wave, new romantics and new technology by drawing on his greatest gift – the art of flamboyance. Like Cab Calloway, Little Richard and Rufus Thomas before him, George Clinton turned his eccentricity into a public spectacle and, with his endless cast of characters, earned a reputation as black music's chameleon.   STUART COSGROVE

Collins. Whereas Parliament's music was an attempt to bring together two different forms of urban soul, George Clinton's other group, Funkadelic (which often featured the same personnel), was an experiment in bringing together two diverse musical traditions.

Dance or die
The name Funkadelic implies a meeting of mighty opposites, an experiment in funk and psychedelia. Along with Sly Stone, Jimi Hendrix and the Oakland-based band War, Clinton tried to find a sound that combined the 'dance or die' principles of black American funk with the expanded consciousness of white rock. Funkadelic's surreal dance music was summed up by one of Clinton's appropriately outrageous album titles: *Free Your Mind And Your*

Above: The boy with stars in his eyes – Bootsy Collins, whose thumping bass lines powered Parliament and several other Seventies funk outfits.

Ass Will Follow (1971). Initially, Funkadelic was an outlet for Clinton's excursions into the world of hard rock and metal music, while Parliament concentrated on experimentation within black musical traditions, but as the Seventies developed the patterns became increasingly confused. Over the years, the Parliament/Funkadelic aggregation was to spawn countless other groups and identities including Bootsy's Rubber Band, the Brides of Funkenstein, Parlet, the Horny Horns, Zapp and the K.9 Corp.

The major contribution that Clinton has made to the history of black music can be

┌───┐
George Clinton/Parliament
Recommended Listening

George Clinton
Computer Games (Capitol EST 12246) (Includes: Get Dressed, Man's Best Friend, Loopzilla, Pot Sharing Tots, Atomic Dog, One Fun At A Time).

Parliament
Mothership Connection (Casablanca CBC 4009) (Includes: P. Funk (Wants To Get Funked Up), Mothership Connection (Star Child), Unfunky UFO, Give Up The Funk (Tear The Roof Off The Sucker), Handcuffs).
└───┘

UNSUNG HEROES

The Crusaders: champions of jazz, funk and soul

ALTHOUGH MAJOR SUCCESS, in the shape of 1979's *Street Life* album and single, was a long time coming for the Crusaders, its eventual arrival was extremely well deserved. Throughout their long and distinguished performing and recording career, the Crusaders have constantly set musical standards for other groups to follow; as a result they are widely acknowledged as supreme professionals of jazz and rock.

The west is the best
Four schoolfriends from Houston, Texas – Wilton Felder (tenor sax), Joe Sample (keyboards), Nesbert 'Stix' Hooper (drums) and Wayne Henderson (trombone) – originally got together as the Swingsters in 1954. Another local lad, Hubert Laws (flute), often joined them on stage as they made their way around the Texas band circuit, while either Wilton or whoever happened to be around at the time helped out on bass. During the next six years or so, the Swingsters adopted names that were designed to be more in keeping with the type of music they were then playing – the Modern Jazz Sextet (history does not record who the other two members of this line-up were), the Nite Hawks and, finally, the Jazz Crusaders. The four then decided to try their luck on the US West Coast.

Although they quickly won the respect of their peers with a series of albums for World Pacific Jazz Records, their music was considered too jazzy for mass appeal. Although collective success proved hard to come by, the four were kept busy either guesting with or acting as session musicians for a wide variety of artists. Joe Sample in particular was very much in demand at Motown, where he regularly appeared on records by the likes of Diana Ross and the Jackson Five. At the end of the Sixties, the Jazz Crusaders duly signed to that label but found little success there.

Dispensing with the 'Jazz' prefix, the Crusaders then signed to Blue Thumb Records. The band's first release for Blue Thumb, the double album *Crusaders I* (1971), quickly outsold each of the previous Jazz Crusaders LPs and carried on the group's policy of bringing in friends to help out, Chuck Rainey playing bass and Larry Carlton, Arthur Adams and David T. Walker sharing the guitar work.

1972's double LP *The Second Crusade* consolidated the group's success, which was further emphasised by *Unsung Heroes* (1973). Aside from its rather apt title, *Unsung Heroes* proved to be one of the key jazz albums of the year, and brought the Crusaders to the verge of the big-time. The band's creative momentum was maintained by a live album, *Scratch* (1974), and

Left: The Crusaders' versatility was typified by Wilton Felder who, in addition to playing sax, was a fine bassist.

yet another double LP, *Southern Comfort* (1974); these releases found the group gaining acceptance on the dance floor.

With Larry Carlton joining as a fifth Crusader and Wilton taking care of bass duties on record, the Crusaders had finally become a settled unit. *Chain Reaction* (1975) showed just how settled they were. By the end of the year, this LP had spent more weeks at Number 1 on the jazz charts than any other album, and had also made

Both keyboard player Joe Sample (left) and drummer Stix Hooper (right) featured with Felder in the Jazz Crusaders' original line-up (below), which also included bespectacled trombonist Wayne Henderson.

an impact on the soul and pop charts. Such was the album's impact that the Rolling Stones had no hesitation in inviting the Crusaders to support them on their 1975 UK tour.

The Crusaders returned to the UK in 1976, this time to tour on their own to the same critical and public acclaim that had greeted them the year before. Their visit followed the release of *Those Southern Knights*, for which the Crusaders had increased in size to become a six-piece band with the addition of Robert 'Pops' Popwell on bass. The album found the group finally using vocals, although none of the band were much more than adequate as singers.

In 1976 Wayne Henderson left the Crusaders to pursue a career as a solo artist and producer. His first solo album, *Big Daddy's Place* (1977), was well received, although overshadowed by his success the previous year with Ronnie Laws, younger brother of flautist Hubert Laws. With Henderson sitting in the producer's chair, Ronnie's debut LP for Blue Note, *Pressure Sensitive*, had become the biggest-selling first LP in the label's history.

While the public waited for a new studio album from the Crusaders to see how the loss of Henderson would affect the band, Blue Thumb's new distributors ABC decided to put together a 'greatest hits' package. *The Best Of The Crusaders* drew upon material from each of the seven preceding albums and was well received.

With the release of *Free As The Wind* in 1977, it was obvious that the departure of Henderson was going to have little or no adverse effect on the band. The LP easily attained the giddy heights reached by *Chain Reaction* two years previously; the group's songwriting was as strong as ever, as was the musicianship.

Larry Carlton left the band in 1978 to pursue a career similar to Henderson's; as a producer he was responsible for a series of highly successful albums by Gap Mangione for A&M, while his own solo LP for Warners, *Larry Carlton* (1978), fared well. The three remaining original Crusaders also decided to release solo albums around the same time. Wilton Felder brought out *We All Have A Star* (1978), Joe Sample followed suit with *Rainbow Seeker* (1978), and Stix Hooper, not to be outdone, came up with his own album, *The World Within* (1979). A joint Crusaders album in 1978, *Images*, with Billy Rodgers on guitar, found the group in a more mellow mood, but this did not hinder its rise up the jazz and pop charts.

Wilton Felder's solo album had introduced a new name to Crusaders fans in lyricist Will Jennings. In 1979 he teamed up with Joe Sample to write the hit 'Street Life', which made Number 5 in the UK, Number 36 in the US. The song's singer, Randy Crawford, was a vocalist for whom

Top right: The Crusaders in concert in 1979, featuring Pops Popwell (bass) and Billy Rodgers (guitar). Right: The group with singer Randy Crawford.

Warner Brothers had great hopes, but who had had little or no commercial success; 'Street Life' changed all that. The 1979 LP of the same name picked up awards around the world, rapidly becoming the Crusaders' most successful album.

Rhapsody And Blues
Randy Crawford's album, *Now We May Begin* (1980), quickly rose up the charts, while a single, 'One Day I'll Fly Away', made Number 2 in Britain. Her belated success with this Crusaders-produced effort prompted Warners to release her previous three albums in the UK.

Bill Withers joined with the Crusaders for 'Soul Shadows' from their 1980 album *Rhapsody And Blues*; although 'Soul Shadows' did not fare particularly well, it helped revive Withers' career. Not long afterwards he teamed up with another big jazz name of the Seventies, Grover Washington Jr, to hit the top spot in the US with 'Just The Two Of Us'.

Over the years, the Crusaders have become expert at breathing fresh life into the flagging careers of other artists: Joe Cocker's vocal performance on the Sample-Jennings song 'I'm So Glad I'm Standing Here Today' was nominated for a Grammy Award, and prompted him to return to recording regularly again.

Two other famous vocalists found their paths crossing the Crusaders' in the Eighties – Bobby Womack, who sang the title track of Felder's second solo LP, *Inherit The Wind*, and 'Someday We'll All Be Free', and B. B. King, who appeared with the Crusaders and the Royal Philharmonic Orchestra at London's Royal Festival Hall in September 1981. This occasion was comemmorated by a double album, *Royal Jam*, released in 1982.

The 1984 album *Ghettoblaster* infused modern funk with their distinctive jazz style. It also featured a new recruit – drummer Leon Ndugu Chancler, replacing Stix Hooper. Chancler's credits include working with Miles Davis and Herbie Hancock and on Michael Jackson's *Thriller* album. Sample and Felder have also followed successful solo careers. In early 1985 Felder, Sample and Chancler joined with Bobby Womack to produce the single 'I'll Still Be Looking Up To You', from Felder's 1985 album *Secrets*.   GRAHAM BETTS

RAP IT UP

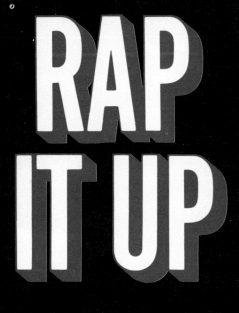

Inset top: Grandmaster Flash hammers out 'The Message'. Above: The Sugarhill Gang, whose 'Rapper's Delight' was rap's biggest hit.

Street-corner jive that brought discos alive

UNLESS YOU WERE a streetwise native New Yorker, the source of the new underground black music that was appearing on disc in 1979 seemed unfathomable. Records like Fatback's 'King Tim III (Personality Jock)' and the Sugarhill Gang's 'Rapper's Delight' were a vibrant amalgam of fast-talking catchphrases and rhymes spoken over stripped-down rhythm tracks. They were called 'rap' and they seemed to spring fully-formed from some hidden tradition.

In the Fifties, the explosion of street-corner harmony groups was immortalised on record by a welter of small independent labels. Entrepreneurs and artists from this period were among the first to spot the potential of the Seventies doowop equivalent. Paul Winley (successful with the Paragons and Jesters), Bobby Robinson (whose labels had hits with Gladys Knight and the Pips, Elmore James and many others), his brother Danny Robinson (whose Holiday label had the Bop Chords) and Sylvia Robinson (singing partner of Mickey Baker on the 1957 US hit 'Love Is Strange') all knew from experience that street culture could be commercial and started signing rapping's nascent stars.

Although the presence of these music-business characters added to the sense of *déja vu* clinging to rap – young kids emerging from youth gangs to shout about fast food, comics, video games, sex, roller skating and, most of all, *themselves* – it also underlines a link back to deeper Afro-American roots. The three Robinsons and Winley were all part of the Harlem scene, one of the great centres of the black music tradition. With the exception of Sylvia Robinson, none of them had made any impact in the increasingly racially integrated disco market and rapping was the opportunity to re-invest in a music closer to rent parties, R&B, jive talking and stairwell production values.

Words on the wireless
On radio, disc jockeys who spread the powerful urban R&B sounds over the airwaves were stars in themselves, introducing records in a high-speed rhyming slang that had developed all the way from African boasting and praise songs through black American oral traditions to the hip argot of Cotton Club bandleader Cab Calloway and the bebop singers. One of the first American DJs, Dr Hep Cat, would galvanise listeners to Austin's KVET with his sports-commentator speed and his crazy couplets: 'If you want to be hip to the tip and bop to the top/You get some mad threads that just won't stop.' Dr Hep Cat, and other DJs, such as 'Poppa Stoppa' (Clarence Hamman Jr) and Georgie Woods ('the guy with the goods'), gave back the 'live' feel to recorded music with their improvised patter.

While the boasting and insulting tradition was kept alive in American music through records like Bo Diddley's 'Say Man' and 'The Story Of Bo Diddley', it took a Jamaican producer, Coxsone Dodd, to find a new direction for DJ jive. On one of his collecting trips to the US – searching out R&B records for his sound system – Dodd became so impressed with the radio style of Jocko Henderson and Dr Jive that he encouraged his own top DJ, Count Machouki, to try out the same techniques. In the competitive world of Jamaican sound systems the idea was rapidly picked

The Sugarhill label – formed by Sylvia Robinson (above) – was quick to spot the commercial potential of rap.

up by rivals, eventually to appear on record in 1965 with Sir Lord Comic's 'Skaing West': 'Come on you cats, get hep, we're going west.'

Although reggae was slow to gain a following in America, a growing Jamaican presence in New York meant that, sooner or later, the Caribbean toasting style of DJ talkover would be recycled into soul. DJ Kool Herc, a resident of the Bronx who had moved from Kingston in 1967, was one of the first of a new generation to popularise the idea of rapping over records. Since the dub records in his collection failed to cut ice with local dancers, he switched to latin-tinged funk. Herc was part of a movement in the Bronx that emerged out of youth gangs, from whom house parties, dancing and writing their street name around town had always been part of their sub-culture.

Graffiti had progressed from felt-tip to spray can and now seemingly covered half of New York; dancing was a dazzling display of head spins and acrobatics called 'breaking' and parties were becoming turntable wars between rival sound systems. Kool Herc's innovations – rapping out street vernacular through an echo chamber over repeated instrumental breaks – were followed by the Grand Wizard Theodor's invention of 'scratching' (manually moving the stylus back and forth in the record groove) and DJ Grandmaster Flash's use of a drum

machine (known as a beat box) in combination with montaged fragments of records. The culture had an identity and a name (hip hop) and its members (called Beat Boys) had a uniform; the sound systems wired their amps into the street lighting and created music from other people's records and their own imaginative skills.

Thus far, hip-hop style was confined to the uptown streets and clubs, but when the Fatback Band heard a tape of DJ King Tim III rapping over a Roy Ayers instrumental, they were sufficiently impressed to record with him. The effect was convincing, probably because Fatback were among the best of the street-funk groups, and the floodgates were opened. Sugarhill, the label formed by Sylvia Robinson, followed up in 1979 with 'Rapper's Delight' by the Sugarhill Gang; for the rhythm track, they stole the memorable bass riff from Chic's 'Good Times' (a huge international hit). It reached Number 36 in the US and Number 3 in the UK.

Both sides up
The arrival of the 12-inch single in the mid Seventies had sparked a terrific advance in disco club mixing and the practice of putting the A-side backing track on the B-side became popular. Endless variations could be rapped over popular tunes, and this led to re-recordings, Jamaican style, over distinctive rhythms – each one a new rap single.

Afrika Bambaataa accomplished one of rap's most daring coups in 1982, by converting Kraftwerk's 'Trans Europe Express' into rap. In collaboration with Streetwise/Tommy Boy producer Arthur Baker and rappers the Soul Sonic Force, Bambaataa put together a record that combined a club atmosphere with hard electronic rhythms, European melodies and a new style of rapping called DJ popping: 'Rockit don't stop it, gotta rockit don't stop/Keep tickin' and tockin', working all around the clock.' 'Planet Rock' was an immediate club and chart hit.

One of the best groups, the Furious Five, who worked with Grandmaster Flash, retaliated the same year with 'The Message', an equally tough rhythm with a lyric that outlined ghetto realities in no uncertain terms: 'They pushed that girl in front of the train/Took her to the doctor, sewed her arm on again/Stabbed that man, right in his heart/Gave him a transplant for a brand new start.' Lines like these, combined with the paranoic hook – 'Don't push me 'cos I'm close to the edge' – were some way from the typical rhymes of the previous three years.

Soon after the release of 'Rapper's Delight', the music industry had begun to predict that rap would soon be finished, yet in the Eighties, its popularity showed no signs of abating. Electro-raps like the Fearless Four's 'Rockin' It', on Bobby Robinson's Enjoy label, and Warp 9's 'Light Years Away' were opening up yet another direction for countless young would-be stars to follow. DAVID TOOP

STARS ON SOLAR

The million-dollar sound of Los Angeles

IT WAS A SIGN of Motown's enormous influence upon popular music in its first quarter-century that virtually every ambitious entrepreneur with his own record label saw himself as the next Berry Gordy Jr, Motown's founder and leading light. Dick Griffey, head of Solar Records, had more reason than most; in less than five years, this native of Nashville made his label, with its related interests in concert promotion, artist management and music publishing, into an organisation second only to Motown itself among black-owned entertainment companies in the US.

Furthermore, Solar (Sound Of Los Angeles Records) became one of black music's most consistently interesting workshops. It launched many hits (over 50 on *Billboard*'s R&B Top Forty between 1975 and 1983) and careers (Shalamar, Lakeside, Dynasty, Midnight Star), creating a distinctive brand of black pop that was very much in tune with the Eighties.

The label's creative architect, Leon Sylvers, also applied Solar's high-gloss, singles-oriented approach to a number of outside acts, including Gladys Knight and the Pips, Evelyn King, the SOS Band, Tavares, the Brothers Johnson and the Detroit Spinners. Sylvers also influenced a new generation of young black producers, such as Kashif.

Heading uptown

Solar was born out of Soul Train Records, a joint venture formed in 1975 by Don Cornelius, host of the popular US black-music TV show 'Soul Train', and Griffey, a former night-club owner and concert promoter who was then booking talent for the programme. Soul Train generated four Top Ten R&B hits between 1975 and 1978, including 'One For The Money' and 'Make It With You' by the Whispers, a veteran black harmony group (managed by Griffey) that had previously recorded for labels such as Janus, Soul Clock and Dore.

Another commercial success was Shalamar's 'Uptown Festival', a medley of 10 Motown oldies that crossed over to make Number 25 in the pop chart. Shalamar began as a studio project produced by Simon Soussan, a stalwart of Britain's Northern Soul scene, but Griffey subsequently formed a performing version of the group, enlisting singer Gerald Brown and two popular 'Soul Train' dancers, Jody Watley and Jeffrey Daniels.

The Soul Train label was dissolved in 1978, and Griffey took its artists – Shalamar, the Whispers and Carrie Lucas, a solo singer who became his wife – to form Solar Records. After a couple of nondescript hits, the company offered the first hint of a distinctive sound in 'Take That To The Bank' by Shalamar, a bright, snappy pop-soul tune strong on harmonies and rhythm. Produced by Leon

Sylvers and Dick Griffey, it became a Top Twenty soul hit in the US and Solar's first UK hit, making Number 20 in the charts.

The label continued to consolidate over the next 12 months, recruiting and developing new acts whose members also became part of its in-house team of song-writers and musicians. There was Lakeside, a nine-man funk combo from Ohio, who made the Top Ten in the R&B charts with 'It's All The Way Live' and *Shot Of Love* (1979); and Dynasty, who charted on both sides of the Atlantic with 'I Don't Wanna Be A Freak', a popular club hit that both parodied and capitalised on the disco style of Chic.

The secret ingredient
Guitarist Stephen Shockley of Lakeside and keyboard player Kevin Spencer of Dynasty became regular members of the Solar rhythm section. Other mainstays were Leon Sylvers (bass), Ernest 'Pepper' Reed (guitar) and Wardell Potts Jr (drums), while Gene Dozier took care of the musical arrangements.

Sylvers gradually became a central figure at Solar. Formerly a member, with others of his family, of the Sylvers vocal group, he began working behind the scenes at Solar in 1978. He and the rest of Solar's creative crew really hit their stride towards the end of the following year, first with Shalamar's 'The Second Time Around' (a US Number 8 pop hit), then with the Whispers' 'And The Beat Goes On'. Each sold more than one-and-a-half million copies in the US, while the Whispers' record went on to reach Number 2 in the UK.

One lesson Sylvers had learned from Motown, consciously or otherwise, was that many of the best black records have an almost tangible *tension* between the various vocal and instrumental components. Motown classics like 'I Heard It Through The Grapevine' and 'You Keep Me Hangin' On' exemplify that quality, and it was no surprise to learn that, as a youngster, Sylvers used to dissect his favourite songs 'to try to find out what made them tick'.

The Motown-Solar likeness extended to Griffey's promotional strategy for his acts. In 1980 he showcased four – Dynasty, Lakeside, Shalamar and the Whispers, with Solar-signed comedian Vaughn West as compère – in the Galaxy of Stars tour, which travelled the US and was seen by over a million people. As with the Motor-town Revues of the Sixties, the performers shared backing musicians, roadies and other support services, minimising running costs and ticket prices.

Griffey's determined, no-nonsense business style was reflected by the company's

Opposite: Dick Griffey, head of Solar.
Right: The Whispers (top) and Shalamar (bottom) were two of the label's biggest acts in the Seventies and early Eighties respectively, while great things were forecast for all-girl group Klymaxx (centre).

small roster of artists and its fine in-house creative unit. A highly influential figure within the American black music community, Griffey was more forthright on political issues than Berry Gordy had ever been, commenting to *Black Enterprise* in 1982 that 'the reason the ghetto is a ghetto is because black folks spend the dollar and that's it. The money doesn't circulate, it evaporates.' He wanted more black people to profit from 'the money our music generates'.

Solar continued to generate money in the Eighties, although crossover acceptance for a number of its most successful R&B releases proved difficult to secure in the US. Major black hits by Lakeside ('Fantastic Voyage', 'I Want To Hold Your Hand'), the Whispers ('Tonight', 'Keep On

Lovin' Me') and Shalamar ('A Night To Remember') did not enjoy corresponding success in the US pop charts.

No such barriers for Shalamar, at least, seemed to exist in the UK. Their 1982 LP *Friends* – a finely-tuned, melodic extension of the original pop sound crafted by Leon Sylvers – yielded a remarkable run of four Top Twenty Hits, 'I Can Make You Feel Good' (Number 7), 'A Night To Remember' (Number 5), 'There It Is' (Number 5) and 'Friends' (Number 12). Jeffrey Daniels was so taken by the band's British success that he decided to settle in the UK; Jody Watley followed suit.

Back in the States, Griffey's company continued to promote its established acts and such Eighties newcomers as Collage, a 10-member band from San Francisco

whose first LP was produced by the Whispers; Klymaxx, an eight-woman Los Angeles outfit produced by members of Lakeside; and Midnight Star, an eight-piece from Ohio, who in 1983 had their first R&B Top Ten hit with 'Freak-A-Zoid'.

Griffey also formed a pop label, Constellation, to which Stevie Wonder associate Bill Wolfer was signed, and undoubtedly he hoped that the return to popularity of Top Forty radio in the United States would allow him to match the crossover achievements of that man from Detroit, Berry Gordy Jr. Like the Motown magnate, Griffey had a clear – if somewhat cynical – approach to the music industry, summed up by his comment that 'this is the entertainment business, not the singing business.'   ADAM WHITE

Below: Solar house producer Leon Sylvers III (third from left) poses with funk quartet parodists Dynasty.

Musicians Only

The post-punk era saw the return of traditional values to rock

As THE DUST SETTLED after the first earth - shaking shock wave of punk rock, the UK music business struggled to overcome a bankruptcy of ideas that had seen the balance of financial power shift dramatically from the established labels. As total record sales declined, major labels had responded by attempting to use their resources to cover all bases, often signing young bands without any knowledge of their strengths and weaknesses or with any clear idea of how to market them.

The pros step forward

Although sales of records by Pink Floyd, Yes and other leviathans of UK rock remained sizeable, the new breed of bands – who often proved to be short-lived – provided little hope for the industry. However, the middle ground was to be filled by a number of bands and singers whose traditional skills of musicianship and songwriting were championed by a new breed of rock entrepreneur. The combination of Sixties skills and Seventies marketing methods

Elvis Costello in 1977 – that year's model. Costello's talent for writing fierce, pointed songs was unrivalled by any of his contemporaries, yet his record sales were inconsistent.

saw these artists emerge as the 'new professionals' of rock.

Musically, paying lip service to changing styles could prove potentially profitable in securing across-the-board success. Thus reggae, which had gained hip appeal during the rise of punk, provided a convenient way of by-passing the high-speed bludgeon of the new wave while identifying with the prevailing fashion. The Police's 'cut-up' technique of interspersing reggae verses with rock choruses was effective for an album's worth of songs, while Elvis Costello followed his first album – *My Aim Is True*, a singer-songwriter's debut in new-wave clothing – with his own reggae pastiche, 'Watching The Detectives'.

Singles were once more the currency of rock – and the budding entrepreneurs of the new wave were not slow to exploit this. Miles Copeland, a UK-based American accountant, replaced the expense accounts of his foundering British Talent Management company with a bread-line-budget operation, in which his group of labels (Faulty, Step Forward, Illegal) released short runs of singles by unknown bands.

Although 'Fall Out', a 1977 single by his brother Stewart's band, the Police, was nothing out of the ordinary, it was successful enough for Miles to bankroll an album. While recording this, the Police 'discovered' reggae and Miles, sensing success, introduced the band to A&M Records, using the profits to set up his own International Record Syndicate label. A&M's resources helped the Police survive the failure of their first three singles, each of which finally entered the UK Top Twenty after intensive re-promotion.

A somewhat different strategy was adopted by Jake Riviera. Having started – and profited from – the new-wave record label revolution with Stiff Records, he startled the rock business by leaving partner Dave Robinson in late 1977 and starting a new label, Radar, in association with Warner Brothers. He took with him Nick Lowe and Elvis Costello and continued to handle their careers with an inspired mixture of hype and marketing – but, even when Warners withdrew their support and Radar metamorphosed into the F-Beat independent, he declined to hive off his bigger acts to provide capital to develop others.

Radio stars

The new professionals of rock understood the need to get radio airplay, and to do so they strived to iron out the rough edges of their sound. Squeeze, for example, had attempted to bolster their new-wave credentials by recording their first album with ex-Velvet Underground man John Cale but it was not until their manager Miles Copeland re-directed them to John Wood, a respected folk-rock producer of Fairport Convention and others, that the classic pop songwriting of Glenn Tilbrook and Chris Difford was afforded the setting it deserved, and a string of classic singles followed. The Police had forged a winning partnership

Below: Miles Copeland, whose astute management of his brother Stewart's band the Police (bottom) helped the group to amass a fortune.

with engineer/producer Nigel Gray that lasted until 1980 and *Zenyatta Mondatta*, while even the Stranglers, a band that had been quick to align themselves with the raw passion of punk, allowed Martin Rushent to tidy up their sound when they first entered the recording studio.

The advent of Dire Straits symbolised the return of the musicianly attributes that had been temporarily eclipsed when punk suggested that a musical vocabulary in excess of three chords was not only unnecessary but heretical. Fronted by Mark Knopfler, a balding, uncharismatic ex-teacher in his late twenties, Dire Straits plainly intended to survive on musical merit alone.

By 1980, traditional values of musicianship had again become acceptable. However, in musical terms, the 'new professionals' of rock rarely managed to sustain the interest of their early work. The Police, like the Who before them, re-formed periodically to produce an album of down-the-line British rock for the American market, the Stranglers typically kept their fans in the dark as to the reasons behind their slide from the aggression of 1977 to the anaesthesia of later releases, while Dire Straits continued to plough their profitable furrow despite several personnel changes behind Mark Knopfler. Only Elvis Costello could be said to have recorded a body of work that, in its variety, bore comparison with that of the Beatles or Rolling Stones, and he was rewarded with inconsistent sales for his trouble.

In all cases, however, the bands made enough money to keep themselves, their record companies and management in early-Seventies style, and as such merit their 'new professionals' tag regardless of musical quality. In Miles Copeland's words: 'The myth of the short lifespan of a rock'n'roll star is over. When you're as big as the Police, you can afford to do things your own way.'

MICHAEL HEATLEY

THE POLICE

Pounding the rock and reggae beat

TOWARDS THE END of the Seventies, as the rock audience became ever more fragmented, the chances of a group achieving the kind of universal success enjoyed by great Sixties bands like the Beatles and the Rolling Stones became increasingly remote. After the punk explosion of 1977, rock took on the appearance of a battlefield, the new-wave insurgents sweeping forward to be met by stern opposition from the old guard, while various other smaller factions – teenybop, reggae and heavy rock – jostled for attention on the fringes.

Against all the odds, however, one group emerged who, while using punk as a flag of convenience, won critical praise for their technical ability, skilfully weaving reggae and rock together to form a highly appealing and unusual music, and looked and sounded attractive enough to capture the hearts and minds of the early-teen audience.

Copeland pounds the beat
The Police were formed by drummer Stewart Armstrong Copeland, born on 16 July 1952 in Alexandria, Virginia, in the United States. His father's work as an agent of the Central Intelligence Agency took the family to Beirut, Lebanon, where Stewart spent much of his childhood. He was later moved to secondary school in England, after which he studied at the University of California in San Diego, majoring in music. Returning to the UK, he landed a job as drummer with Curved Air, a progressive British group fronted by vocalist Sonja Kristina (with whom he was to become romantically involved) and managed by Stewart's brother, Miles Copeland.

This was invaluable experience, and it taught Copeland a great deal about the music business. Curved Air were caught in what had become a familiar situation for many bands at that time. High overheads and big record-company advances due for repayment made the band's operation cumbersome and unprofitable, while their music had become increasingly staid and bland in response to business pressures which dictated safety as a preferable option to experimentation.

By late 1976, the band's lease of life was nearly up. Copeland, a restless man with boundless energy, found the group thoroughly frustrating and had not failed to notice the new mood of urgency that the fledgling punk movement was starting to bring to the music scene. The idea of forming his own group on more radical, basic lines was never far from his thoughts – he even had a name, the Police – but he lacked suitable recruits. It was after a gig at Newcastle Polytechnic in December 1976 that various members of Curved Air went to see local jazz-rockers Last Exit – a band which featured a vocalist/bass player by the name of Sting.

Gordon Matthew Sumner was born 2 October 1951 in Wallsend, Northumberland. Of above-average intelligence, athletic, and good looking, the young Sumner clawed his way up the educational ladder, shedding most of his Tyneside accent on the way. After an aborted university course, he trained successfully for a teacher's certificate in English and music. Between 1971 and 1974 he played in a variety of local Newcastle groups, picking up the nickname Sting when he turned up to a session wearing a black and yellow sweatshirt reminiscent of a wasp. The most accomplished of these various bands was Last Exit. 'Sting had then what he has now,' Copeland said. 'This fantastic presence. It was really pretty obvious that he had enormous potential.'

Copeland persuaded Sting to move down to London and form a band with him, although he had no guitarist lined up. That vacancy was filled by Corsican-born Henry Padovani, a novice musician, but as Copeland put it: 'He knew a few chords and he was really enthusiastic and when he'd had his hair cut and stuff he really looked the part.' The trio played sporadic gigs round the capital and recorded a single, 'Fall Out', that was released in May 1977 on the independent Illegal record label and sold encouragingly considering it had no national distribution.

But Sting was constantly at loggerheads with Padovani's lack of musicianship: 'Henry was deadweight in that sense. I just couldn't write guitar parts for him because he couldn't play them,' he said. At this point, Copeland was writing most of the group's material and Sting's interest in the band was hanging by a thread. The final piece of the jigsaw fell into place, however, when Sting and Copeland were invited by former Gong bass-player Mike Howlett to play a one-off gig in Paris with a group called Strontium 90; the group's guitarist was to be Andy Summers.

Completing the trio
Andrew James Summers was born on 31 December 1942 at Poulton-le-Fylde near Blackpool, Lancashire, and through the Sixties and Seventies he served one of the longest apprenticeships to rock superstardom on record. He was a founder member, with Zoot Money, of the R&B-oriented Big Roll Band, which changed into the psychedelic Dantalion's Chariot in 1967. He had spells with Soft Machine and the New Animals before studying classical guitar for three and a half years at San Fernando State College in the US. During the Seventies, he toured with Tim Rose, Neil Sedaka and David Essex before joining the Kevin Coyne Band in 1975 and, a year later, Kevin Ayers' band.

The Strontium 90 project was his first introduction to Copeland and Sting; a few weeks later he went to see them as the Police, with Padovani, playing at the Marquee. Summers joined in on the encore, and later suggested he should join the group. They played two gigs as a quartet before Padovani departed, later to turn up as guitarist with Wayne County and the Electric Chairs, and later in his own Flying Padovanis. The new Police trio made their debut at Birmingham's Rebecca's Club on 18 August 1977.

Men for all seasons
Summers, Copeland and Sting were all seasoned, highly skilled players inspired by the energy and attitude of punk. This caused much suspicion, both from punks on the one hand, who saw the group as lacking street credibility, and from the establishment on the other, who put it down as a blatant attempt at jumping the bandwagon. Neither view was correct, and what eventually turned people's heads was the group's successful merging of musical styles to produce a sound that was uniquely their own – particularly their use of reggae.

Freed from the technical limitations of Padovani's guitar-playing, Sting now felt more inclined to contribute to the songwriting; indeed, from this point he took over from Stewart Copeland as the group's principal composer. One of his earliest contributions was 'Roxanne', the number that finally persuaded Miles Copeland that his young brother's 'little punk band' might be worth investing some time and effort in after all.

Miles, against his own better judgement, had already lent the band enough money to start work recording an album, even though they did not have a recording contract. The plan was to produce the album as cheaply as possible and sell it independently. They calculated that if they sold 5000 copies they could break even. (The resulting album, *Outlandos D'Amour*, was eventually in the UK album charts for 96 weeks.)

Miles Copeland took 'Roxanne' to A&M Records, who agreed to release it. The fact that the Police were not paid an advance enabled Copeland to negotiate a highly favourable royalty deal, sowing the seeds of an enduringly profitable relationship with the record company. 'Roxanne' was released in April 1978 and, although not a hit, it created a stir of interest. This encouraged A&M to release a follow-up single, 'Can't Stand Losing You', in August, and to take up an option to release *Outlandos D'Amour* at the end of 1978. 'Can't Stand Losing You' nudged into the Top Fifty, and a groundswell of popular support was building. The Police were burning on a slow fuse when Miles Copeland announced his most audacious move. Unknown and unsigned outside the UK, the band were going to tour America.

In 1978, the idea of an unknown British group touring the US challenged conventional thinking. The three members of the band plus roadie/soundman Kim Turner flew to the States on Laker Airways' cut-price Skytrain, carrying their instruments as hand luggage. The four of them, travelling in one van with all their equipment, did a tour of East Coast clubs – 23 gigs in 27 days – raising interest in every town they visited and promoting 'Roxanne', which had been released as a one-shot single and which now began to get radio play, reaching Number 32.

The band made money out of the tour, showing that a streamlined, low-overheads approach could work just as well, if not better, than traditional methods. They returned to Britain with renewed vigour and the added kudos of success in the States. In April 1979, a re-released 'Roxanne' made the UK Top Twenty, *Outlandos D'Amour* entered the album charts, and the Police never looked back.

The appeal of the Police was wideranging, and many different factors accounted for their phenomenal success. Musically, what they did for reggae was the same thing that the Rolling Stones and other British bands in the Sixties had done for the blues; they took the basics of a specific ethnic music and built a hybrid pop style around it, thereby contributing to the central core of musical fusions that define what rock music actually *is*. They delivered this 'rock-reggae' with a brash energy derived from their admiration of punk, and operated with a taut vitality which Summers ascribed, in part, to the fact that they were a trio: 'Our three egos are all very strong . . . and in a three-piece the roles are more dynamic. From experience I know that in quartets you tend to pair off. There's a tensile strength in a trio.'

The three blonde heads, a look originally adopted for the band's participation in a chewing-gum commercial, provided the perfect visual tag, while the faces beneath were pretty enough – in Sting's case, classic heart-throb material. Thus, as well as the regular rock audience, they inherited a teenybopper market that had lain dormant since the days of the Bay City Rollers and David Cassidy.

It's the chemistry
Live, the Police opted for an exuberant, spontaneous excitement in their music. Sting, with his knee-bending left-to-right sway (a mannerism subsequently adopted by bass players the world over), would encourage the audience to engage in handclapping and much celebratory chanting and singing along. Copeland, all sticks and lanky limbs, provided a barrage of explosive percussion, while the lithe and compact Summers would occasionally forsake his normally serious pose to leap about the stage. The three possessed a certain indefinable chemistry common to all the great groups.

The final factor in their favour was having the entreprenurial skills of the Copeland empire to back up their talents, and the will to do business their own way. Their second album, *Reggatta De Blanc* (1979), was recorded in four weeks at a cost of between £6000 and £9000, a fraction of the amount lavished on, for instance, the second album by those doyens of streetcredible new wave, the Clash. Produced by the Police and their engineer, Nigel Gray,

Reggatta De Blanc went to Number 1 in the UK, as did the singles taken from it, 'Message In A Bottle' and 'Walking On The Moon'. During 1979 the Police sold five million singles and two million albums – but unlike most bands, they had never been in debt to a record company.

Policing the East
In 1980, their finances and future secure, Miles Copeland decided the time was right to extend the Police legend to all parts of the globe. He organised a world tour, but one that took in all sorts of places that had never even seen a rock band before. In January they set off on a two-and-a-half-month stint that took them to four continents, playing 37 cities in 19 countries including India, Egypt, Venezuela and Hong Kong. An accompanying BBC film crew recorded much of the trek for posterity, and the resulting television presentation, 'Police In The East' ensured that the folks back home were not unaware of the band's achievements.

A third album, *Zenyatta Mondatta* (1980), was recorded in some haste; despite receiving almost universal critical censure and even some negative comments from the band themselves, it appears, in retrospect, to be a remarkable, raw distillation of the Police's art. Perhaps because of the speed with which they were written and recorded, the songs tended to be concise, rather blunt statements. 'Shadows In The Rain' and 'Voices Inside My Head' were both neurotic, rhythmically-dominated atmosphere pieces that amply demonstrated the band's propensity for growth and their willingess to experiment and extemporise.

Besides boasting the usual beguiling melodies, 'Driven To Tears' and 'When The World Is Running Down, You Make The Best Of What's Still Around' signalled a new maturity in Sting's lyrical concerns. Perhaps the world tour had alerted him to troubles external to his own emotional traumas, which had been the predominant theme of most of his previous work. 'Driven To Tears' was a particularly poignant comment on token reactions to coloursupplement portrayals of Third World suffering, coming as it did from the pen of a young millionaire: 'Seems that when some innocents die/All we can offer them is a page in some magazine/Too many cameras and not enough food/This is what we've seen.'

The two singles taken from the album were the rather twee 'Don't Stand So Close To Me', the Police's third UK Number 1, and the curiously lambasted 'De Do Do Do, De Da Da Da', an untypically humble and precisely articulate testament to the power of words both as instruments of influence and deception. It was also the single that re-established their popularity in America, being their first US chart entry since 'Roxanne'.

For the rest of 1980 the band toured North and South America, but the sustained effort had begun to take its toll

and dates in Australia and New Zealand were cancelled due to illness. For the first half of 1981 the three members went their separate ways, re-assembling in July in Montserrat to start work on their fourth album, *Ghost In The Machine*, with a new co-producer in Hugh Padgham. Despite their increasing prosperity and a more relaxed recording environment, it turned out to be a rather joyless album, although it reached Number 1 in the UK regardless. The nagging calypso of 'Every Little Thing She Does Is Magic' contrasted with an overall greyness exemplified by the dour 'Invisible Sun', a single whose accompanying video, incorporating scences from strife-torn Northern Ireland, was banned from BBC television.

In the same way that the Police had learned from and avoided the business mistakes of their predecessors, they also paid heed to the dangers of being taken over by the rock treadmill of non-stop writing, recording and touring. In 1982 they broke off and renewed themselves as individuals. Despite the intense workload of the Police, Sting had managed over the years to build up a promising film acting career. His first role was as the Ace Face in *Quadrophenia* (1979), a part he had landed before the Police made their breakthrough. He subsequently appeared in *Radio On* (1979), *Brimstone And Treacle* (1981) and a television production, 'Artemis 81' (1981).

In parallel with his Police career, Stewart Copeland made occasional mysterious appearances in the guise of Klark Kent. His first single, his own composition called 'Don't Care', on which Copeland played all the instruments and sang, reached Number 48 in the UK chart in August 1978, two months before the Police made their first ever chart entry with 'Can't Stand Losing You'.

May the force be with you
A second Kent release in 1980, a six-track 10-inch disc, was not successful and the stranger dropped from sight. Copeland subsequently pursued his various interests, which included polo and raising ponies, and ventured into filming. Andy Summers, meanwhile, developed his talent for photography; his work was exhibited in America, and his first volume of photographs, *Throb*, was published in October 1983. He also collaborated with guitarist Robert Fripp to produce an album of enigmatic instrumentals, *I Advance Masked* (1982).

In 1983, after a year's absence that gave rise to the inevitable rumours of a split, the band stormed back into the public eye with the *Synchronicity* album, which produced a Number 1 single in 'Every Breath You Take', plus two further hits, 'Wrapped Around Your Finger' and 'Synchronicity II'. Their success remained undiminished, and indeed reached new heights in the US, where both album and single lodged at Number 1. With their eye for the masterstroke, they staged a concert at New York's

Shea Stadium, once the scene of the historic Beatles appearance, further fuelling the Police legend.

At the movies

1983 finished with tours of America and Britain, and the announcement that 1984 was likely to be another 'year off'. Sting appeared in the BBC's *Threepenny Opera*, and in *Dune*, an epic film version of the science fiction classic. In addition to continuing his photography and undertaking further collaborations with Robert Fripp, Summers was also planning to go into acting. Having written the soundtrack for Francis Ford Coppola's film *Rumblefish*, Copeland had completed filming a punk documentary featuring the Anti-Nowhere League, entitled *So What*.

Predictably, Sting was to prove the group's shining solo star, with hit albums *The Dream Of The Blue Turtles* (1985), the live *Bring On The Night* (1986) and the UK chart-topping double *Nothing Like The Sun* (1987). But a brief Police reunion in 1986 resulted in a rerecording of 'Don't Stand So Close To Me' reaching Number 24 in the UK, while the hits LP *Every Breath You Take* made Number 1 UK/7 US that Christmas.

Combining a flair for the unusual with meticulous attention to detail, the Police were indisputably the major rock act of the early Eighties.
DAVID SINCLAIR

Top, from left: 'Softly softly catchee monkey' seems to be the slogan of this rickshaw policeman! On stage (centre), the Police are somewhat more active, while their world travels took them as far off the rock tour circuit as Egypt (top right) and India. Right: Stewart Copeland takes a break from the drums, twanging Sting's electric double bass. Centre right: The globetrotting Flying Squad pay a visit. Below right: Robert Fripp and Andy Summers unmasked after their 1982 album collaboration. Far right: The magic that is Sting.

THE POLICE
Discography to 1983

Singles
Fall Out/Nothing Achieving (Illegal IL 001, 1977); Roxanne/Peanuts (A&M AMS 7348, 1978); Can't Stand Losing You/Dead End Job (A&M AMS 7381, 1978); So Lonely/No Time This Time (A&M AMS 7402, 1978); Message In A Bottle/Landlord (A&M AMS 7474, 1979); Walking On The Moon/Visions Of The Night (A&M AMS 7494, 1979); Don't Stand So Close To Me/Friends (A&M AMS 7564, 1980); De Do Do Do, De Da Da Da/A Sermon (A&M AMS 7578, 1980); Invisible Sun/Shambelle (A&M AMS 8164, 1981); Every Little Thing She Does Is Magic/Flexible Responses (A&M AMS 8174, 1981); Spirits In The Material World/Low Life (A&M AMS 8194, 1981); Every Breath You Take/Murder By Numbers (A&M AM 117, 1983); Wrapped Around Your Finger/Someone To Talk To (A&M AM 127, 1983); Synchronicity II/Once Upon A Dream (A&M AM 153, 1983).

Albums
Outlandos D'Amour (A&M AMLH 68502, 1978); *Reggatta De Blanc* (A&M AMLH 64792, 1979); *Zenyatta Mondatta* (A&M AMLH 64831, 1980); *Ghost In The Machine* (A&M AMLK 63730, 1981); *Synchronicity* (A&M AMLX 63735, 1983).

The menacing music of the men in black

PUNK'S ROLL CALL in early 1977 identified the Sex Pistols as depraved vandals, the Clash as a cadre of urban guerillas, the Damned as slapstick-and-horror caricatures and the Jam as angry retro-Mods. The Stranglers, clad in black, were the movement's sneering cynics, callous and pestilential. Long after the Pistols and the Jam had broken up, the Damned had become a punk music-hall joke and the Clash had turned to internecine warfare, the Stranglers continued to pump out their intoxicating rhythms, although their songs of the Eighties were fragrant and summery by comparison with their old ones. Perhaps this was a sign of changing times, or perhaps the Stranglers, despite appearances to the contrary, had always yearned to find 'true love and happiness in the present day'.

It has been argued – with some justification – that the Stranglers were never punks in the first place – drummer Jet Black was pushing 40, while most of the band had obtained degrees. Yet although the Stranglers' origins clearly predated punk, their success was definitely related to it, as was their subversive stance, their arrogance and their tendency towards violence. Their physical aggression was manifested most strongly by bass player Jean-Jacques Burnel, at times practising his black-belt karate on those fans foolish

Left: The men in black, from left Dave Greenfield, Jean-Jacques Burnel, Jet Black and Hugh Cornwell. Above: The Stranglers give a typically gripping performance.

enough to spit on him. Born in Notting Hill Gate, London, of French parents, Burnel had taken up martial arts when a much-bullied pupil at school in Guildford, Surrey. He later went to university, becoming both an accomplished classical guitarist and a would-be Hell's Angel.

Late in 1974 Burnel met singer-guitarist Hugh Cornwell and drummer Jet Black at their Guildford flat, situated

Although Burnel's abuse of journalists brought the Stranglers a lot of media attention, the band's main contribution to punk's shock tactics was Cornwell's wearing of a T-shirt bearing a rude word at a Rainbow concert. However, Cornwell was quite clear about the importance of punk to the group's success: 'What the punk scene has made (record companies) do is turn round and see what's right under their noses. The punk onslaught on the business made our music acceptable.'

In February 1977, the Stranglers' first single '(Get A) Grip (On Yourself)' made Number 44 in the UK charts. April saw the release of *Rattus Norvegicus*, which reached Number 4 in the LP listings.

Macho men

If the twilight romanticism of 'Goodbye Toulouse' and the urban broodiness of 'Hanging Around' showed one side of the Stranglers, the album also revealed their most controversial quality. This was their deep, apparently ingrained misogyny. Four or five tracks violently abused women, with the lascivious bump and grind of 'Peaches', the leering 'Princess Of The Street' ('She's a queen of the street /What a piece of meat') and the scathing 'London Lady' being particularly offensive. The Stranglers' macho posturing, as moronic as that of the worst heavy-metal bands, lapsed so readily into bathos, however, that it seemed obviously satirical.

These deliberately crass songs, most of them boasting fine melodies and all of them beautifully played, smacked of sexual rejection by women of impotent men (hence the ferocious 'Ugly' by way of revenge). This was hardly something the oh-so-virile Stranglers would admit themselves, but it was arguable that they were striking attitudes on behalf of their predominantly male audience rather than espousing a sexist cause.

Just six months – time enough for UK Top Ten hits in 'Peaches' and 'Something Better Change' – elapsed before the Stranglers released their second album, *No More Heroes*, in September 1977. This reached Number 2 in the charts, while its fierce title track became a Number 8 hit single. *No More Heroes* was heavier and more acerbic than its predecessor. Its misogyny was nastier still in 'Bring On The Nubiles' and 'Something Better Change', while the ghoulish 'Peasant In The Big Shitty', the baleful 'English Towns' ('There is no love inside of me/I gave it to a thousand girls') and 'I Feel Like A Wog' offered dangerous visions of alienation. On a more personal level, 'Dagenham Dave' paid homage to a faithful friend and fan of the band who had died.

By 1978, the Stranglers had established themselves as one of Britain's major live bands in Britain. Their concerts were always savage affairs, with the burly Black and the sullen Greenfield behind their respective batteries of drums and keyboards and Burnel and Cornwell out front. This sinister pair – the unsmiling,

above Black's liquor store and ice-cream factory. Cornwell, from Kentish Town, North London, had ready chemistry at Bristol University, taught biology and formed various bands, most notably Johnny Sox in Sweden. Once back in England, he had teamed up with Black through a music-press advertisement. With Burnel on bass, the three called themselves the Guildford Stranglers, rehearsed in a Scouts' hut and travelled to gigs in Black's ice-cream van.

In May 1975, the Stranglers recruited Brighton keyboard-player Dave Greenfield and proceeded to notch up over 200 live dates in the next 18 months. They appeared regularly at London rock venues such as the Nashville and the Hope and Anchor and then supported Patti Smith on her 1975 UK tour. The band were thus already on the verge of success when punk exploded on the music scene.

Opening doors

Unlike many of the new punk bands, the Stranglers were actually quite accomplished musicians. With Greenfield's rasping organ-work quickly earning the band a spurious (but very street-credible) comparison with the Doors, United Artists hastily signed the Stranglers for £40,000 in December 1976.

sardonic Cornwell, film-star handsome with a lick of hair dripping over his forehead, and the scowling Burnel – shared the vocals; Hugh's was the crueller voice, Jean-Jacques' the breathier one.

Despite 'Do You Wanna' and 'Nice 'n'Sleazy' (a Number 18 hit that, when played live, usually featured a stripper), the tracks on the Stranglers' third LP, *Black And White* (1978), showed them turning away from crude machismo towards more apocalyptic themes ('Curfew' and 'Enough Time') and rampant xenophobia in 'Outside Tokyo' and 'Sweden (All Quiet On The Eastern Front)'. Burnel contributed the rousing but fascistic 'Death And Night And Blood (Yukio)', inspired by the Japanese writer Yukio Mishima who had committed ritual suicide. There was also the poppy 'Hey! (Rise Of The Robots)', the anti-militaristic *blitzkrieg* of 'Tank' and an oblique love song in 'Toiler On The Sea'. Musically, the Stranglers were on especially brilliant form, and the album made Number 2 in the UK charts. The band followed this success with a sinister and highly acclaimed reworking of Dionne Warwick's hit 'Walk On By' which reached Number 21 in August 1978.

The Stranglers lost some momentum with the release, in March 1979, of the disappointing *Live (X Cert)* which failed to capture the menace of the band in performance. However, after a long break from recording, the band were back on form with their fourth studio LP, *The Raven*, which appeared in October 1979.

The tender touch
The Raven departed from both the Stranglers' characteristic Gothic organ sound – Greenfield creating some exquisite new effects with synthesisers – and their tendency towards punk power chords. Though Cornwell drily denounced California, Australia and Iran respectively in 'Dead Loss Angeles', 'Nuclear Device' and 'Shah Shah A Go Go', the songs had little of the old malevolence. Burnel gave a beautiful, insidious vocal performance on the slow-moving 'Don't Bring Harry', an anti-heroin song with weeping guitar lines, while Greenfield's voice could be heard on the chilling 'Genetix'. There were signs, moreover, that the Stranglers were matching their keener sound with a new reflective tenderness. 'The Raven' was informed with a new optimism born of past sadness: 'Fly straight with perfection/Find me a new direction/You never realised the things they said/We'll never realise until we're dead.'

'Baroque Bordello', meanwhile, was a romantic view of sex and 'Duchess' – a Number 14 hit single – was a moving pop song from Cornwell recalling an old love. This rich, experimental LP became the Stranglers' own favourite – four years later, their live sets still included up to five songs from *The Raven*.

The following year, 1980, was a bad one for the band. A concert in Nice that ended in a riot incurred the wrath of the French

authorities; the Stranglers were accused of incitement and threatened with 20-year jail sentences. Although all charges were later dropped, Cornwell was then jailed in England for three weeks for possessing drugs. A third calamity then befell the band – the theft of all their gear during an American tour. Heavily in debt, the band hovered on the verge of a break-up.

A gentle disguise
They successfully overcame this crisis in their affairs, however, and in February 1981 released *The Men In Black*, a quasi-religious concept album about shadowy, parasitic aliens from outer space. It was their lightest effort yet and lacked conviction, apart from two strong instrumentals in 'Waltzinblack' and 'Turn The Centuries, Turn'. *La Folie*, released in November of that year, was much more consistent and could be seen as a development of styles first glimpsed on *The Raven*.

Although some of the music on *La Folie* sounded comparatively gentle, evil lurked behind its innocuous façade. Nowhere was this more true than in the mellow title track, whose lyrics, sung in French, told the true story of a Japanese student who murdered and then devoured his girlfriend. 'Tramp', 'Let Me Introduce You To The Family', 'How To Find True Love And Happiness In The Present Day' and 'The Man They Love To Hate', were among the LP's highlights, while the airy, delicate 'Golden Brown' received massive airplay on BBC Radio One and even Radio Two, and became the band's biggest hit single, reaching Number 2 in January 1982. In the same reflective vein, the single 'Strange Little Girl' made Number 7 in July of the same year.

In 1983 the group released *Feline*, which provided them with a hit single in 'European Female' – yet another meditative song, it indicated that women had attained at least some degree of dignity and beauty in the eyes of the Stranglers. 1986's *Dreamtime* and 1988's *All Live And All Of The Night* saw punk's survivors trimming their sails for the Nineties with a substantial fan following intact.

Apart from various solo excursions such as Cornwell's *Nosferatu* (1979), Burnel's *Euroman Cometh* (1979) and Burnel and Greenfield's *Fire And Water* (1983), the Stranglers remained a tight, self-sufficient working unit. They progressed from punk vermin to Eighties punk philosophers, while their albums have always been fresh and provocative and their concerts exciting. The Stranglers, in rock-music terms, belie their own adage that there are 'No more heroes any more.'   GRAHAM FULLER

> **The Stranglers**
> **Recommended Listening**
>
> *Rattus Norvegicus* (EMI FA 3001) (Includes: Peaches, Goodbye Toulouse, London Lady, Ugly, Down In The Sewer, Hanging Around); *The Raven* (Liberty/United Artists UAG 30262) (Includes: Longships, The Raven, Ice, Nuclear Device, Duchess, Genetix).

As the Stranglers grew in confidence, their image as backyard rockers (above) gave way to the sinister aura exemplified by the artwork of their 1979 LP The Raven *(left). On stage, the brooding presences of Burnel and Cornwell (below and right) remained the main focus of attention.*

I'M NOT ANGRY

Did success mellow Elvis Costello?

A CRUEL SNAPSHOT, the picture of Elvis Costello on the back sleeve of his first album *My Aim Is True* (1977) was a perfect visual metaphor for the realities its songs so ruthlessly described. Elvis looked disfigured, crippled by staggering humiliations: his smile was mirthless, his body twisted and grotesque. On the record's songs, Costello seemed to be looking up from the basement in a frenzy of jealousy and rage. 'I'm not angry!' he announced with a sneer, but it was a monstrous deceit. No one had ever sounded as furious as Elvis Costello on *My Aim Is True*. And anger was an emotion that was to permeate Costello's career from then on.

Zero hour

Elvis Costello was born Declan MacManus in London on 25 August 1954, the son of Ross MacManus, formerly vocalist with the Joe Loss dance band. When his parents divorced, Declan took his mother's surname and moved with her to Liverpool; during the early Seventies, he played in various garage bands.

Moving back to London, Costello worked as a computer operator at the Elizabeth Arden cosmetic factory in Acton, and in the evenings fronted a pub-rock band called Flip City or played folk clubs as D. P. Costello. Accumulating a repertoire of original songs, he decided to approach the record companies, looking for a deal. Stubbornly individual, he regularly by-passed the traditional avenues of approach: instead of submitting demo tapes to companies, Declan would turn up at their offices with his guitar and insist upon playing his songs to the baffled A&R men, whose only response was rejection.

Inevitably, he was drawn to Stiff Records, a label that had already become a haven for unorthodox talents. In early 1977, Jake Riviera signed Costello to Stiff, re-named him Elvis, and put him and his songs into a studio with Nick Lowe, by now established as the label's house producer. Stiff subsequently released the anti-fascist broadside 'Less Than Zero', followed by 'Alison', an intense and beautiful love ballad; the charts remained immune to the singer's charm, however.

In July, Costello's debut album emerged. Produced by Nick Lowe on a budget so slim that it was almost invisible, *My Aim Is True* was a circumscribed reflection of Costello's abilities. Still something of an apprentice behind the mixing desk, Lowe could not fully accommodate the wide vocabulary of musical styles that Elvis' songwriting already embraced. More critically, the support provided by US West Coast country-rockers Clover, then resident in London, was largely functional and often a little dull. Neither the production, nor the group's playing, adequately illuminated the fierce rage and indignation of the songs – although tunes like 'Miracle Man', 'Blame It On Cain', 'I'm Not Angry', 'Mystery Dance' and 'Pay It Back' positively hummed with scathing venom.

By the time the LP was released, however, it was obvious that Costello had already outgrown its restrictions. Riviera realised that Elvis needed a band to fuel his volatile cocktails and brought together the Attractions.

Pete Thomas, formerly with Chilli Willi and the Red Hot Peppers (whom Riviera had managed) was brought in on drums and Bruce Thomas (no relation), an ex-member of British country-rockers Quiver, joined on bass. Keyboard-player Steve Mason, quickly re-christened Nieve, was the final addition. Classically trained, Nieve was untutored in rock'n'roll; at his audition, he downed a bottle of sherry, confessed that the only rock acts he had ever heard were Alice Cooper and T.Rex, and promptly passed out. But his presence in the band would be crucial: from the shrieking Farfisa organ landslides on *This Year's Model*, through the grooving Booker T.-like organ surges of *Get Happy!!*, to the florid keyboard-work of *Trust*, Nieve's intelligent versatility would be almost as important to the sound developed by Costello and the Attractions as the leader's own voice and songs.

On 26 July 1977, Elvis was arrested for busking outside the London Hilton where CBS were holding their annual conference (this was the first of many outrageous stunts devised by Riviera to promote Costello, who was later to sign to Columbia in America). That evening, having been

Opposite: 1977-vintage Elvis on the release of My Aim Is True *– 'a cruel snapshot'. Right, from top: The angry young man loosens his tie (centre) and finds a voice (bottom).*

bailed out, Elvis played his first London date with the Attractions, at Dingwalls. The next night, the Attractions played the Hope and Anchor in Islington before a packed and excited crowd. When Costello opened a residency at the Nashville later that summer, police were called in to control the rowdy fans.

Elvis was *hot*, and in November he had his first UK Top Twenty single. 'Watching The Detectives' was recorded before the formation of the Attractions with the Rumour's rhythm section, Andrew Bodnar and Steve Goulding; it seethed with paranoid sexual frustration. More complex, more startling than the explicit detonations of *My Aim Is True*, the song was released to coincide with the opening of the first Stiff Tour, a trek that combined the various talents of Costello, Nick Lowe and Dave Edmunds, Larry Wallis and Ian Dury. As the tour swung through the country, 'Watching The Detectives' clambered up the charts to Number 15. But a rift had already occurred in the Stiff camp: realising that managing both Costello and the Stiff label would be too much of a handful, Riviera had decided to split, signing Nick and Elvis to Andrew Lauder's emerging Radar label.

War in peace
Riviera was clearly impatient to get Costello across to America to capitalise quickly on the success of *My Aim Is True*. The US lapped him up, but Costello was not to prove an easy catch. Bristling with belligerent energies, Costello made many American critics and much of his nascent public distinctly uneasy. Requests for interviews were sneeringly scorned; hackles rose and were quickly shaved by Costello's barbed tongue and Riviera's mischievous business tactics. Invited to appear on TV's prestigious 'Saturday Night Live', Costello had planned to play 'Less Than Zero' – but after a few desultory bars, he and the Attractions swung gleefully into the vitriolic 'Radio Radio', a song that viciously attacked the authoritarian supremacy of the radio networks.

If *My Aim Is True* described Elvis Costello to his public, the follow-up LP, *This Year's Model*, *defined* him for them. Released in March 1978, and prefaced by the spiteful thrust of '(I Don't Want To Go To) Chelsea' (a Number 16 hit in the UK), *This Year's Model* was played by the Attractions with a scorched-earth intensity structured around the shattering impact of Pete Thomas' sensational drum attacks.

Costello's songs, meanwhile, were a gushing tide of derision and contempt, unsparing condemnations of everything about contemporary society – and himself – that disgusted him, from the superficial fripperies of fashion, of which he was now a part, to the lurking threat of fascism. With a savage relish, Costello confronted private and general anxieties and phobias, prejudices and conceits.

Above: Elvis punches out time on stage. Above right: Costello's Attractions, from left Bruce Thomas, Pete Thomas, Elvis and Steve Nieve. Right: Horns back the band in 1983. Below: Rocking against racism, 1978.

Not since Dylan's 'Positively Fourth Street' had a performer's lyrical and musical skill so lethally matched his malicious intent as it had done on *This Year's Model*. But if it represented a peak in Costello's career, it also gave him no opportunity to climb down.

In February 1979, Elvis Costello released his third album, *Armed Forces*. This provided a UK Number 2 hit in the anti-mercenary song 'Oliver's Army', but the remainder of the LP struck many observers as somehow glib, transparently tuneful but eventually trite. Apart from the sinister elegance of 'Green Shirt', the oddly affecting opening couplets of 'Two Little Hitlers' and the supremely aching poise of the incandescent 'Accidents Will Happen', the record seemed empty.

Mr Happy

In the Spring, Costello toured America once more and, frustrated by the strict, predictable routines of another promotional campaign, he began to lose his temper with increasing regularity. Events came to a head on the night of 16 March when Elvis, the Attractions and their entourage found themselves sharing the bar at the Holiday Inn in Columbus, Ohio, with Stephen Stills, Bonnie Bramlett and their respective bands. A drunken argument ensued and a fist-fight quickly followed. Costello was alleged to have described Ray Charles as 'an ignorant blind nigger' and James Brown is said to have been dismissed by him with similar racist contempt.

Costello emerged from the fiasco as a sinister bigot. Although he claimed he had just been ferociously drunk, the damage had been done; New York gigs were picketed by anti-racism activists, most of whom had conveniently forgotten Costello's public demonstration of his sympathies for the Rock Against Racism movement at London's Brockwell Park not a year earlier. It would be 18 months before he toured the US again.

Back in England that summer, Costello produced 2-Tone ska revivalists the Specials' debut album, and in the autumn began work on a new album of his own. As the giant Warner Brothers concern had been losing money on Radar, they had decided to wind the company down; therefore, Riviera came out with his own label, F-Beat. The new project's first release was Costello's single 'I Can't Stand Up For Falling Down', a cover of an obscure B-side by Sixties soul stars Sam and Dave, which reached Number 4 in the UK charts. The second release was the album *Get Happy!!*

The irony of the title was an indication of the extent to which Costello had been affected by the traumas of the previous year. These were the songs of someone attempting to come to terms with everything that had gone wrong in both his life and his career. *Get Happy!!* was also a stylistic diversion. Elvis had obviously been listening to a lot of Sixties soul music and the album was played at the clip of a classic soul revue, 20 songs packed into 47 minutes, only one tune clocking in at more than three minutes.

Gloom still coloured Costello's general outlook, however and, after the obligatory tour to promote the album, he temporarily parted company with the Attractions. While he was deliberating upon his future, Columbia in the States released *Taking Liberties*, a 20-track collection of alternative takes, rare flipsides and previously unavailable snippets of a rare kind of genius at work: with a few minor alterations, the compilation was released in the UK as *10 Bloody Marys And 10 How's Your Fathers*.

By the end of 1980, Elvis was firing again on most of the old fronts. 'Clubland', one of his finest ever shots, was an explosive trailer for a new album. A brooding, highly charged epic that panned across a nervous social landscape with an unrelenting stare, 'Clubland' was altogether too fraught and taunting for the Christmas market and made only Number 60 in the UK singles chart. But more bewildering than the chart failure of 'Clubland' was the distinct lack of success enjoyed by *Trust*, the album that followed it in January 1981. Although the LP reached Number 9, it remained in the lists for only seven weeks.

This must have been a source of painful concern for, although Elvis was later tempted to dismiss it, *Trust* was a formidable achievement. It had its share of miscalculations, but the variety and sheer excellence of its best moments – 'Clubland', the peerless 'New Lace Sleeves', the ominous 'Big Sister's Clothes' – finally established Costello as an heir to a tradition of songwriting broader and deeper than any of his rivals could accommodate.

Soon after *Trust*, Costello went to Nashville. Elvis had always loved country music – in 1980 he had duetted with the legendary George Jones on a single, 'Stranger In The House' – and had decided to record a country-rock album of his own. Produced by C&W veteran Billy Sherrill, *Almost Blue* was full of deliciously emotional performances and his readings of 'Good Year For The Roses' (a freak UK Top Ten hit single), 'Too Far Gone' and Gram Parsons' 'Hot Burrito No 1' (here re-titled 'I'm Your Toy') were quite impeccable. Strangely, considering its somewhat parochial appeal, *Almost Blue* fared better than *Trust* in the British LP charts, reaching Number 7.

Costello ushered in 1982 with an extravagant New Year's show at London's Royal Albert Hall, at which he and the Attractions were augmented by the weight of the Royal Philharmonic Orchestra. Meanwhile, on either side of Christmas and the New Year, Elvis had been ensconced in London's AIR Studios, recording his seventh album. Eventually released in July, *Imperial Bedroom* was obviously intended to be regarded as a 'major statement'. A suite of songs looking for a vague narrative thread, the record was overproduced and overblown. Costello's voice was everywhere, overdubbed and overbearing; Steve Nieve's keyboards were uncharacteristically prominent, while Pete Thomas' mighty drumming was reduced to a flat pat.

The record reached Number 6 in the UK album charts nonetheless, but a simultaneous succession of singles found the public stubbornly resisting every attempt Costello made to get a hit. Not that he was putting out much that anyone could honestly cheer: there was a gruff stab at Smokey Robinson's 'From Head To Toe' and there was the wretched 'Party Party', which Elvis had written as the theme for an equally wretched movie. Virtually his only good work during this period was 'Shipbuilding', a song inspired by the Falklands War, which was co-written with Clive Langer for Robert Wyatt.

By the spring of 1983, Costello's commercial standing was at a low ebb, and a new strategic assault was clearly needed to revive his career. In May, he pulled off the required coup by recording an acerbic, state-of-the-nation address called 'Pills And Soap', the lyric of which continued the theme of social concern and acid commentary that had characterised 'Shipbuilding'. In a move that would have done credit to the early Stiff marketing campaigns, Costello personally delivered copies of the record – which was credited to 'The Imposter' – to selected recipients, flattering them into a sense of conspiracy. The record reached Number 11 in the UK in July.

Punch The Clock, the Clive Langer and Alan Winstanley-produced album which followed at the end of the month, was another major disappointment, however. 'Every Day I Write The Book', a Top Thirty single, was one of Costello's most cultured songs but was the only genuine light on a very dim collection.

Clocking off

In the usual ironic way of things, the same public that had overlooked *Trust* flocked to the stores for *Punch The Clock* – perhaps because of the massive publicity that the new LP received. 1984 saw the release of another Imposter single, 'Peace In Our Time'. An LP, *Goodbye Cruel World*, followed. It was an entertaining set of well-crafted songs, but broke little new ground, although it produced a hit single in 'I Wanna Be Loved'. Two completely different albums in nine months, the gentle *King Of America* (recorded as the Costello Show) and the vicious *Blood And Chocolate* (both 1986) showed he still had the capacity to surprise. ALLAN JONES

JOAN ALONE

Joan Armatrading: rock's solitary solo star

'MY BAND TRAVEL with me, but I'm not one for rushing off to parties or to clubs after my own concerts. I just go to my hotel room and shut myself in. I prefer it that way. I enjoy thinking and reading and I do a lot of reflecting. People think that I'm lonely, but I'm not. I've always been this way and I'm happier alone.'

Joan Armatrading's own summary of her touring habits has revealed her character as the antithesis of the brash personality popularly associated with the archetypal rock star. Yet beneath the unassuming exterior of this non-smoking, teetotal vegetarian slumbers an ego strong enough to have sustained her through a formidable number of solo releases – some excellent and all executed with great firmness of purpose.

While a characteristic attention to detail has been evident in her every song, this very scrupulousness has seemed to prevent her touching true depths of emotion or heights of passion, except on a handful of recordings. Although she has claimed her songs have not been especially autobiographical, they have tended to be written in the first person and dealt with affairs of the heart. Despite all this apparent soul-searching, she has remained an elusive, shadowy figure. Armatrading's stature as a major rock artist has thus resided not so much in her limited lyrical talents as in her remarkable ability to blend various musical styles – folk, gospel, jazz-funk, soul, reggae and, increasingly in the Eighties, rock – into a tasteful mélange that appealed to a mass audience.

Hair and there
Joan spent her first seven years on the island of St Kitts in the West Indies, where she was born on 9 December 1950, before moving with her family to Birmingham, England. Although her father was a part-time musician, he did not encourage her musical ambitions. She recalled: 'My father used to hide his guitar on top of the cupboard where I couldn't reach it. On reflection this might have been so that it wouldn't get damaged – but he certainly never pushed me towards music.'

While performing in a production of *Hair*, she met lyricist Pam Nestor. The two began writing together and won a recording contract with Cube Records. Yet despite the jolly 'one-big-happy-family' artwork of their subsequent LP – *Whatever's For Us* (1972), produced by Gus Dudgeon – arguments arose between Pam, Joan and Cube when Joan's name alone was featured on the sleeve. It took Joan three years to extricate herself from her contract with Cube and sign to A&M. Her first LP for that label was the Pete Gage-produced *Back To The Night* (1975), a solid rather than inspired work whose most adventurous track, the jazzy 'Cool Blue Stole My Heart', showcased her fine grasp of rhythm and dynamics.

Her combination of confident musicianship and personal diffidence quickly endeared her to the public when she began touring to promote the LP, backed by fellow A&M band the Movies. She became the special favourite of feminist audiences, the mid Seventies being a time when there were few female performers with Joan's authority operating in British rock.

To the limit
Her growing confidence was clear on the next LP, *Joan Armatrading* (1976). This was her first collaboration with noted producer Glyn Johns, whose previous credits included the Eagles and Gallagher and Lyle; the album yielded a Number 10 UK hit single in 'Love And Affection' and made Number 12 in the LP charts. Johns had assembled a superb collection of musicians, including guitarist Jerry Donahue and drummer Dave Mattacks of Fairport Convention and bassist Dave Markee. Johns later commented in John Tobler and Stuart Grundy's book *The Producers* that *Joan Armatrading* was the best album he had ever made and remembered Joan as 'the most extraordinary talent ... she made me aware of things, of tastes I didn't even know I'd got. The most odd person to work with, who finds it totally impossible to verbalise her thoughts ... Very difficult indeed, but wonderful.'

The chemistry that existed between Johns and the comparatively inexperienced Armatrading was just as evident on their subsequent studio recordings, *Show Some Emotion* (1977) and *To The Limit* (1978), which respectively made Number 6 and 13 in the LP charts. Despite the excellence of the backing musicians Johns employed – on *Show Some Emotion* the list included Georgie Fame (electric piano), John 'Rabbit' Bundrick (organ), Mel Collins (sax) and Henry Spinetti (drums) – the music was firmly based around the driving funk or languorous picking of Joan's acoustic guitar. Her singing on these albums was to remain her best, her voice moving effortlessly from muscular, melancholy sonorities to hit high notes of surprising delicacy and purity.

Show Some Emotion contained numerous fine tracks, in particular the ballad 'Willow' and the jazzy 'Get In The Sun' and

'Kissin' And A Huggin''. *To The Limit* showed Joan exploring reggae rhythms, notably in 'From The Bottom To The Top' and was punchier and less sentimental.

After recording a live album, *Steppin' Out* (1979), Johns and Armatrading parted company, both perhaps feeling that they needed a rest from each other. Joan's subsequent releases, 1980's *Me Myself I* (produced by Richard Gottehrer), 1981's *Walk Under Ladders* and 1983's *The Key* (both produced by Steve Lillywhite) each represented conscious moves on her part towards a rockier sound. *The Key* yielded a Top Twenty single, 'Drop The Pilot', in the UK charts.

Shouting to be heard

After Xmas 1983's compilation *Track Records,* 1985's *Secret Secrets* and the following year's *Sleight Of Hand,* betrayed a certain sameness. But at last 1988 saw Armatrading, now producing herself, back in some style with *The Shouting Stage.* Now competing with a near-soundalike in Tracey Chapman whose career had flourished in the interim, she remained an honest and consistent performer who never sold out to commercial pressure.

ALASTAIR DOUGALL

Joan's move from gentle, acoustic funk (opposite) to electric rock (right) reflects her growing assurance as a live performer in the Eighties (below).

> **Joan Armatrading**
> **Recommended Listening**
>
> *To The Limit* (A&M AMLH 64732) (Includes: Bottom To The Top, You Rope You Tie Me, Let It Last, Am I Blue For You, Your Letter, Barefoot And Pregnant); *Track Record* (A&M JA 2001) (Includes: Love And Affection, Me Myself I, Drop The Pilot, Down To Zero, Show Some Emotion, Heaven).

Sultans of Swing

The relaxed expertise of Dire Straits

OF ALL THE BANDS to have emerged in the late Seventies, none appeared more out of step with the times than Dire Straits. Launched at a time when rock was still experiencing the after-effects of punk and led by balding guitarist Mark Knopfler, Dire Straits appeared to have been caught in a late Sixties/early Seventies time warp. As far as the group were concerned, the punk shake-up that occurred in London in 1976 might never have taken place.

Although their image was decidely unfashionable, Dire Straits had one thing going for them in the climate of the late Seventies British rock scene: they *were* a 'street band'. Like Nick Lowe and Ian Dury, Dire Straits had served their musical apprenticeship on the London pub-rock scene that had evolved in the Seventies, although it should be added that the group had not spent years slogging round this grimy circuit. Apart from drummer Pick Withers, the members of the band – Mark Knopfler (lead guitar and vocals), David Knopfler (rhythm guitar) and John Illsley (bass) – were relative newcomers to the music scene.

Swinging into action
Mark Knopfler (born 12 August 1949) was in his late twenties when the band was formed in 1977, and had had time to absorb and utilise a number of influences, most notably those of Bob Dylan and that quintessentially 'laid-back' songwriter-guitarist J. J. Cale. Knopfler was certainly no callow youth: by the time he formed Dire Straits in 1977, he had already pursued two separate careers – as a journalist and as a teacher. His skills as a songwriter and guitarist had had time to mature fully; those who listened to Dire Straits' first single, 'Sultans Of Swing', found it hard to believe that the record was not the work of a seasoned performer.

'Sultans Of Swing' began life as a £120 demo disc that found its way on to the playlist of Charlie Gillett's 'Honky Tonk' show on Radio London. The Sunday lunchtime show kept abreast of all that was new and exciting on the London scene, as well as featuring top American talent like Ry Cooder and sundry other rhythm and blues performers. The record immediately caused a minor sensation, and within weeks numerous record company representatives, chequebooks at the ready, were to be found hovering in the wings at Dire Straits' increasingly well-attended gigs.

Released on Phonogram's Vertigo label, 'Sultans Of Swing' took time to gain the public's attention, but finally claimed its deserved place in the charts, reaching Number 9 after the appearance of the band's first LP. *Dire Straits* (1978) made Number 5 in the UK album chart, and within a year the band had conquered virtually all of the world's major record markets. They became particularly

Opposite: Mark Knopfler 'steps out and bends one'. Above: Dire Straits in 1983, from left Knopfler, John Illsley, Hal Lindes, Terry Williams and Alan Clark. Williams replaced original drummer Pick Withers after 1982's Love Over Gold.

popular in the US, their music being more acceptable to American radio programmers than much of what was then emanating from the British record industry.

Future Dire Straits releases would be criticised for their blandness, but 'Sultans of Swing' remains a classic single. As the record shows, Dire Straits were largely a vehicle for Knopfler's guitar-playing and songwriting. Although unquestionably American in feel, 'Sultans Of Swing' sought to evoke Knopfler's experiences of London. He had been born in the capital, but had spent most of his life in the north of England; he thus saw London with the fascinated eyes of an outsider. 'Sultans Of Swing' was a paean to a bunch of South London amateur jazz musicians who could blow with the best. 'Wild West End', also from the first album, represented another of Knopfler's slices of London life.

Dire Straits' first album had been produced by Muff Winwood, the elder brother of multi-talented instrumentalist-singer Steve Winwood. For their second album, the group decided to enlist the service of veteran R&B producers Jerry Wexler and Barry Beckett. This was not a particularly surprising move, as several critics had

claimed that Winwood had made the group sound too 'clean'. It was assumed that Wexler and Beckett, who had worked with the greatest R&B artists, would beef up Dire Straits' sound.

In fact, the ensuing album, *Communiqué* (1979), differed little from its predecessor, underlining the impression that Dire Straits were fundamentally bland on record. Knopfler's playing was as tasteful as ever, although the LP's songs were not as strong as those on the first LP (a single release, 'Lady Writer', only made Number 51 in the UK) and thereby emphasised his limitations as a vocalist. Their sound seemed to ensure them continued commercial rewards, however, and *Communiqué* sold just as well as the first LP.

Keys to success
During their brief career, Dire Straits had never needed to struggle to find their own identity. Knopfler's musical vision, derivative though it was, was perfectly in focus from the beginning. While this led to the band's immediate success, it also meant that after a relatively short time, Dire Straits had become too stylised for their own good. But changes seemed imminent when second guitarist David Knopfler, tired of being in his elder brother's shadow, decided to leave the group and go solo.

For Dire Straits' next album, *Making Movies* (1980), Mark Knopfler decided to play all the guitar himself and bring in keyboard-player Roy Bittan, from Bruce

2199

Above: Dire Straits in full swing. Right: David Knopfler, who left the band to pursue a solo career.

Springsteen's E Street Band, to freshen up the group's music. Bittan's playing certainly helped *Making Movies* to be a more satisfying album than *Communiqué*. It reached Number 4 in the UK charts and contained one of Mark Knopfler's finest compositions, the 'street-light' ballad 'Romeo And Juliet' (a Number 11 hit). For Dire Straits' 1980 tour, Hal Lindes played rhythm guitar, with Alan Clark on keyboards.

Going for gold
Meanwhile, Knopfler's stock as a guitarist continued to rise; he played on some prestigious sessions, working with Dylan on *Slow Train Coming* (1979) and with Steely Dan on *Gaucho* (1980). The influence of Dylan and, it must be added, Bruce Springsteen, had always loomed large in Knopfler's songwriting and playing. These American influences were more apparent than ever on *Love Over Gold* (1982), the LP that took Dire Straits to new commercial heights, reaching Number 1 in the UK album charts.

Love Over Gold – which featured Mike Manieri on vibes and Ed Walsh on synthesiser – was the group's best album since their auspicious debut. Produced entirely by Knopfler, who by this time had taken up residence in New York, it was a meticulous piece of work. Side one consisted of just two songs – the heroic 'Telegraph Road', which owed more than a little to Springsteen, and the atmospheric 'Private Investigations', a UK Number 2, whose classical overtones recalled the second part of Fleetwood Mac's 1969 hit 'Oh Well'. Another highlight was the quirky humour of 'Industrial Disease', the shortest track on the LP at two seconds under six minutes.

Knopfler has provided music for the films *Local Hero* (1983), *Cal* (1984) and *Comfort And Joy* (1984). He also co-produced and played on Bob Dylan's *Infidels* (1983) and on Aztec Camera's *Knife* (1984). 1984 saw the release of Dire Straits' best-selling live double LP *Alchemy*, while the 1985 album, *Brothers In Arms*, saw the band back in the limelight and embarking on a major tour – covering 25 countries and lasting one year.

STEVE CLARKE

Dire Straits
Recommended Listening

Dire Straits (Vertigo 9102 021) (Includes: Sultans Of Swing, Wild West End, Six Blade Knife, Water Of Love, Lions, Down To The Waterline); *Making Movies* (Vertigo 6359 034) (Includes: Tunnel Of Love, Romeo And Juliet, Solid Rock, Les Boys, Hand In Hand, Expresso Love).

Coventry Calling

A grey English city set a nation dancing to the 2-Tone beat

2-TONE WAS MORE than a record label, more than a new dance craze, more than the flagship of a ska revival. It was something more contagious: a dance-floor manifesto, a serious attempt to radicalise the conservative imperatives of the music business. For two giddy years its music swept virtually everything before it.

The unlikely architect of this guerrilla campaign against contemporary complacencies was a former art student named Jerry Dammers, a misfit whose energy, determination and idealism inspired the emergence of his group, the Specials, and the 2-Tone movement he built around them. Working with a single Revox tape recorder in the front room of his flat in Coventry, Dammers started shaping songs that were a synthesis of punk's fierce rage and the infectious rhythmic clatter of ska, a music that had first become popular with the Mods in Britain and then the skinheads in the late Sixties.

From those early sessions in Dammers' front room emerged a succession of groups, which culminated in the Special AKA (later called the

Left: Jerry Dammers, the eccentric founder of the Specials and 2-Tone. Top: The Selecter were one of his label's first signings.

Specials), who filled the support slot on the Clash's 1978 On Parole Tour. By the end of the tour, Clash manager Bernie Rhodes wanted to manage the Special AKA: a contract was drawn up, but Dammers refused to sign it. The Special AKA returned to Coventry for a bleak winter spent penniless and unemployed, but they somehow managed to finance the release of 'Gangsters' on the group's own label 2-Tone; 5000 copies were distributed by the independent label Rough Trade, enough to qualify for a chart placing and a deal with Chrysalis soon followed.

Sounds like success

The Specials were soon joined on the label by the Selecter, a project which had now developed from Neol Davies' original song of the same name on the B-side of 'Gangsters' to become a band. The two bands and their managers ran 2-Tone jointly, and the label soon took off. 'Gangsters' reached Number 6, and was quickly followed by Madness' tribute to Prince Buster, 'The Prince', and the Selecter's 'On My Radio'. The Specials were soon back in the Top Ten with 'A Message To You Rudy' and 'Nite Klub', while the Beat charted in November with their 2-Tone debut, 'Tears Of A Clown'.

2-Tone fervour reached a thrilling peak that October when the Specials, Madness (now on the Stiff label with their own debut LP to promote) and the Selecter embarked on an extensive British tour. The following February, the Selecter's striking debut album appeared. Its sound was harder than that of the Specials; songs like 'Black And Blue' and the Number 16 hit 'Three Minute Hero' added a nervy, almost paranoid edge to the 2-Tone sound.

After one single release on 2-Tone, Madness had moved to Stiff, where they were soon to run up a seemingly inexhaustible succession of hits. The Beat quit, too, to found their own label, Go-Feet. They were less abrasive than the Specials, but similarly committed to the causes of racial harmony and nuclear disarmament.

In less amicable mood, the Selecter quit 2-Tone in July 1980. Believing that corporate success was stifling new talent, and encouraging a stereotyped 2-Tone sound, they originally tried to wind up the label – and, when that failed, they quit it. Signing directly to the parent company Chrysalis, the Selecter changed their line-up slightly and released their second LP, *Celebrate The Bullet*, in the spring of 1981.

Dammers continued to try to develop the label, releasing records by veteran Jamaican trombonist Rico, the Swingin' Cats and the Bodysnatchers. The latter, an all-woman band, played a set full of ska classics like '007', 'Monkey Spanner' and 'Double Barrel', and their first 2-Tone single, 'Let's Do Rock Steady' reached Number 22 in March 1980. But for the first time, 2-Tone releases were struggling in the UK charts. The Bodysnatchers split after the failure of their second single, 'Easy Life', a record which represented the more serious, explicitly political direction some of the band, including vocalist Rhoda Dakar, wanted to pursue. Rhoda went on to join the Special AKA, while other members of the band formed the nucleus of the pop-oriented Belle Stars.

Opposite: Buster Bloodvessel, extrovert frontman of Bad Manners, who toured with and played the same kind of ska-influenced music as 2-Tone bands like the Bodysnatchers (inset top left) and Madness (inset top right). Above: The 2-Tone logo and those of the principal groups associated with the label.

The Specials' political affiliations had always been with the left, but their music and image had often attracted right-wing skinheads whose presence was often unsettling and wildly at odds with the group's views. During the original 2-Tone tour there had been a serious outbreak of violence at Hatfield Polytechnic. Early Madness gigs were also a focus for outbreaks of violence that were as upsetting to the groups as for anyone caught up in the often brutal mayhem. The autumn tour realised many of the Specials' worst fears: there were mini-riots at Cardiff and Newcastle that left them in despair. Then in Cambridge a small war broke out. Jerry and Terry intervened, trying to stop the fracas, and were subsequently charged and fined for 'using threatening words and behaviour'.

Disgusted and disillusioned, the Specials decided on a brief sabbatical. Jerry worked on production for Rhoda Dakar, the Apollinaires and the Higsons; drummer Brad formed Race Records, Neville launched a label called Shack and Roddy Radiation gigged with his own band, the rockabilly-based Tearjerkers. In March 1981, *Dance Craze*, an ill-defined documentary film on the 2-Tone phenomenon, was released.

But if time was running out for the Specials, their finest moment was still to come. That summer there were riots throughout Britain, youthful discontent turned to violence and open confrontation with authority. With ironic timing, the Specials released 'Ghost Town', a moving lament for a country that was caving in under the pressure of its own frustrations. To add to the irony, the single went to Number 1 during the week of the Royal Wedding.

Back to basics

No one could have realised how close the Specials were to disintegration. Returning from an American tour, Terry Hall, Lynval Golding and Neville Staples split to form the Fun Boy Three, while Jerry, reverting to the name the Special AKA, built a new group around himself and Brad. By the time they released the astonishing, abrasive 'War Crimes' (1982), the population was already dancing to the glossy beat of the new teen idols; the public wanted escapist entertainment, and the social concerns championed by Dammers no longer seemed relevant to them.

As the 2-Tone star waned, Madness went from strength to strength. All white and – despite their commitment to the Campaign for Nuclear Disarmament – largely apolitical, they fitted into the popular entertainment mould in a way the more abrasive Specials never could. Bad Manners, although they were never on the 2-Tone label, also appropriated the ska sound, linking it with knockabout humour to produce UK Top Ten hits like 'Can Can' (1981) and 'My Girl Lollipop' (1982).

In the circumstances, it was unsurprising that, when 2-Tone released the compilation LP *This Are 2-Tone* in November 1983, it was seen largely as an epitaph to the label. But Jerry Dammers could look back upon what he achieved with the Specials unembarrassed by compromise. 2-Tone was an idea that was realised, an ideal that flourished: the music it promoted would not easily be forgotten.

ALLAN JONES

Dance music for the new depression

THE ORIGINAL SPECIALS were the inspiration behind 2-Tone, one of the most exciting musical movements of the Seventies. The group harnessed the powerful energy of punk to the tuneful, good-natured music of pre-reggae Jamaica: calypso and ska. The music that resulted was thoroughly infectious, particularly live; their enthusiasm was the perfect antidote to the gritted-teeth nihilism of punk rock. But the fun was far from mindless; from their earliest days, the Specials manifested a concern for social problems like unemployment, poverty, racism and violence that particularly affected their bleak Midlands home town of Coventry. The multi-racial line-up presented evidence of their ideas in action.

Ska-faced gangsters

Formed in mid-1977, the band went through a number of names, the best-known being the Coventry Automatics, before eventually settling on the Special AKA for their first release. The line-up consisted of Jerry Dammers (keyboards), John 'Brad' Bradbury (drums), Roddy 'Radiation' Byers (lead guitar), Lynval Golding (rhythm guitar), 'Sir Horace Gentleman' Panter (bass) and vocalists Neville Staples and Terry Hall.

The sound of the group was a remarkable fusion of seemingly disparate elements: a solidly swinging rhythm section peppered by stinging work on the rims of the drums from 'Prince Rimshot' (Brad); Roddy Radiation's venomous punk guitar breaks; Dammers' mad fairground organ and Terry Hall's sardonic vocal delivery set against the rumbustious toasting of Neville Staples. The group's outrageously energetic stage act gathered such momentum that, by the end of most gigs, a large proportion of audience had joined the band on stage. The live sound was often fleshed out by brass, most notably the golden horn of veteran Jamaican trombonist Rico.

The Clash's Joe Strummer was an early convert to the Special sound, and he arranged for the band to get the support slot on his band's 1978 tour of the UK. It was a dispiriting experience for the band facing a series of audiences whose narrow-minded preconceptions about punk led them to react with indifference, if not outright scorn.

Having failed to make friends and influence people, the Special AKA withdrew to reconsider their strategy. This resulted in the birth of the 2-Tone project, intended more as a musical manifesto than a mere record label. A former art-college student, Dammers designed the famous 2-Tone logo himself and, in a statement announcing the birth of the label, it was heralded as an operation 'run by musicians instead of businessmen'.

It was also Dammers who wrote the first single, a savage attack on the music business entitled 'Gangsters' with an appropriate nod to Prince Buster, an inspirational figure to both the Specials and Madness. The whole band pooled all their available cash to get the single recorded. They did not have enough money to record a B-side so this was eventually provided by Neol Davies, a local musician who was billed as the Selecter and would later form a band of the same name and sign to 2-Tone. A distribution deal was struck with noted independent outfit Rough Trade in March 1979, and the single was released shortly afterwards.

Rick Rodgers, the band's shrewd new manager, organised a small tour of London's clubs, places where the band could start to gather a following and hope to attract some interest from the major

Above: The original Specials pose in Ghost Town. Left: A Nite Club audience lap up the group's energetic stage act.

By the beginning of 1980, the Specials were in a position to undertake their first visit to the US, where they played a long series of dates, some supporting the Police, others as headliners in their own right. But the first signs of things to come were apparent when several members of the band admitted that their heart was not in some of the later dates.

Live and dangerous

Back in the UK, however, the story was utterly different. To compensate fans for their absence in America, the Specials released a live EP, *The Special AKA Live*, which contained a version of 'Too Much Too Young' from the debut LP. The other four songs on the EP were all cover versions of reggae stompers much favoured in the original skinhead era of the late Sixties – 'Guns Of Navarone', 'Long Shot Kick De Bucket', 'Liquidator' and 'Skinhead Moonstomp'. Live EPs had rarely done well in the UK charts, but 'Too Much Too Young' raced to the top, giving the band their first Number 1. 1980 continued to be a successful year for the band, with further hits in 'Rat Race' (Number 5), 'Stereotype' (Number 6) and 'Do Nothing' (Number 4).

The group also negotiated the traditionally thorny problem of a second LP with *More Specials*, an album in a more relaxed vein than its predecessor. Recorded in Coventry and produced by Jerry Dammers and Dave Jordan, the album featured the usual supporting cast plus guests Kix Thompson from Madness on sax and vocalist Rhoda Dakar – from yet another 2-Tone signing, the Bodysnatchers – who was featured on 'Pearl's Cafe'. *More Specials* received mixed reviews but managed, nevertheless, to reach Number 5 in the UK album charts.

1981 provided the Specials with their finest moment. While riots raged in Liverpool and Manchester that summer, the new Specials single, 'Ghost Town', was a

record companies. Both aims were admirably fulfilled. 'Gangsters' reached Number 6 in the UK singles charts at the end of July and enthusiastic record labels started bidding for the right to distribute 2-Tone. The group eventually signed a deal with Chrysalis which promised them complete freedom from interference in both the artistic and commercial fields.

The Selecter and Madness were soon releasing singles on the new label, and along with the Specials, these two groups played a 40-date tour of the UK in the autumn of the same year and all three appeared on the same edition of BBC-TV's 'Top Of The Pops' in November.

Their first LP, released at the end of 1979, was called *Specials* – the group had now dropped the 'AKA' tag. Elvis Costello had been another of the group's early converts, and he offered his services as producer. It was a strong set, mixing songs with a strong social content – 'Stupid Marriage' and 'Concrete Jungle' – with thoroughgoing rave-ups in 'Do The Dog' and 'Nite Club'. It also provided the band with a second Top Ten hit with the skanking 'A Message To You Rudy', released as a single in October 1979. Rico and Dick Cuthell played horns on the album.

Far left: Lynval Golding (left), Terry Hall (centre) and Neville Staples left the Specials in 1981 to form the Fun Boy Three. Below: The Fun Boy Three on stage shortly before their split in 1983. Left: The regrouped Special AKA pose for the cover of their 1983 single 'Bright Lights'/'Racist Friend'.

chilling view of the deeper problems behind the troubles, set to an eerily relaxed rhythm and memorable melody. Its topical theme seems to have struck a chord; the single soared to Number 1.

But, at the height of their success, the Specials were falling apart. Close observers of the group had always been aware that acrimonious dissent was never far from the surface. The most consistent reason given was Dammers' authoritarian control of the band; he was almost single-handedly responsible for their success in songwriting terms.

On the Specials' return to the UK in October 1981, Terry Hall, Lynval Golding and Neville Staples announced their departure from the group and the formation of the Fun Boy Three. A short time after this, Roddy Radiation decided to leave to form a rockabilly outfit called the Tearjerkers. The final blow to what remained of the original line-up came when bassist Horace Gentleman, who had joined the religious sect Exegesis, fell out with Dammers and left.

While Jerry Dammers and Brad attempted to put the pieces of a new band together, the Fun Boy Three were off and running with a debut single less than a month after their departure from the Specials. Entitled 'The Lunatics Have Taken Over The Asylum', its doom-laden rhythms belied the group's name, but nevertheless gave them a UK hit single at Number 20. Television appearances showed that the trio had abandoned all traces of their former band's wild antics.

Early in 1982, Terry Hall spotted an all-female trio called Bananarama, and in the spring the two trios combined to produce a Number 2 hit single with their version of the Thirties standard 'It Ain't What You Do It's The Way That You Do It'.

Worth waiting for

The connection was continued when the Fun Boy Three contributed backing vocals to Bananarama's hit single 'Really Saying Something'. Their debut album, *The Fun Boy Three* (1982), also had vocal backing from Bananarama and instrumental help from the Swinging Laurels; the single 'The Telephone Always Rings' reached Number 17, while their version of Gershwin's 'Summertime' made Number 18.

But the group suffered a serious setback when Lynval Golding was viciously attacked with a broken bottle at a Coventry night-club; this nearly cost him his sight and caused the cancellation of the group's first UK tour. Furthermore, the Fun Boy Three's last single of the year, 'The More I See (The Less I Believe)', which addressed itself to the problems in Northern Ireland, failed to become a hit after receiving minimal radio airplay.

The release of *Waiting*, the Fun Boy Three's second LP, dispelled any doubts about the group's future: the eight months spent writing material for the LP were seen to have been worth it. Produced by Talking Head David Byrne and with

arrangements by ex-Ravishing Beauty Nicky Holland, *Waiting* offered a series of strong songs convincingly played in a wide variety of styles, from uptempo tracks like 'We're Having All The Fun' to reflective pieces such as 'Things We Do'. The LP also gave the group a Number 10 hit single in 'Tunnel Of Love'.

In 1983 the Fun Boy Three undertook successful tours of both the UK and America and had a UK Top Ten hit with the single 'Our Lips Are Sealed'. Half way through that year, however, the group split up, and Terry Hall formed The Colour Field.

By any other name . . .

Meanwhile Dammers and Bradbury had reverted to their original name of the Special AKA, and had rebuilt the group. Three vocalists were involved: Rhoda Dakar, who had previously recorded and gigged with the Specials; Stan Campbell, another Coventry native who had been with a late incarnation of the Selecter, and Egidio Newton, a session vocalist and one-time member of Animal Nightlife. Gary 'Roobish' McManus and John Shipley were recruited to play bass and guitar.

The new line-up first appeared on vinyl backing Rhoda Dakar on her harrowing and powerful anti-rape polemic 'The Boiler' (1982). The record proved too strong for radio play, and consequently the single only struggled into the lower reaches of the chart. The next release showed that Dammers was in no way disconcerted by the lack of public response. Entitled 'War Crimes', it was a damning indictment of the Israeli involvement in the massacre of Palestinian refugees in Lebanon. Two further singles, the double A-side 'Bright Lights'/'Racist Friend' and 'Free Nelson Mandela' (both 1983), confirmed that the Special AKA would settle for nothing less than acceptance on their own terms. All failed to succeed in the charts. In 1984 the band's first album *In The Studio* was released. The following year Dammers produced a benefit single for the Namibian Support Committee's Repression and Political Prisoners Campaign. Adapted from a Namibian song, 'The Wind Of Change' featured vocals by Robert Wyatt and Zimbabwean Richard Muzira and backing by Lynval Golding and Annie Whitehead. Regardless of pop fashions, it seemed that Jerry Dammers and his band would continue to confront contemporary problems in what they considered the most appropriate musical setting. PETER CLARK

The Specials
Recommended Listening
Specials (2-Tone CDL TT 5001) (Includes: Concrete Jungle, Little Bitch, Too Much Too Young, Do The Dog, A Message To You Rudy, Monkey Man).

Fun Boy Three
Recommended Listening
The Fun Boy Three (Chrysalis CHR 1383) (Includes: Sanctuary, The Lunatics Have Taken Over The Asylum, It Ain't What You Do It's The Way That You Do It, Way On Down, I Don't Believe It, Best Of Luck Mate).

THE BIRMINGHAM BEAT

Pop, ska and reggae from the Go-Feet crew

WHEN A BIRMINGHAM band called – with characteristic simplicity – the Beat made Number 6 in the UK charts with their debut single 'Tears Of A Clown' in January 1980, they registered the fifth consecutive Top Twenty hit for the new 2-Tone label. The cheerful, energetic sound of this first single set the Beat apart from the mainstream of the 2-Tone movement, and conveyed an enthusiasm that, while it lasted, established the band as one of the brightest hopes of the post-punk music scene.

The Beat certainly stood out from the dour 2-Tone stereotype presented by the Specials and the Selecter. Their two fresh-faced frontmen, the blond Dave Wakeling and rasta-turned-punk Ranking Roger and their dancing 'Beat Girl' logo reflected a romantic side that gave them more teen-pop appeal than their 2-Tone contemporaries. The logo was devised by local artist Hunt Emerson, whose distinctive artwork adorned most of the Beat's record sleeves.

Brum boys

Although closely associated with their Birmingham base, the Beat initially came together in the Isle of Wight, where Midlanders Dave Wakeling (born 19 February 1956) and guitarist Andy Cox (born 25 January 1956) were working in 1978 making solar panels. They met local bassist David Steele (born 8 September 1960)

and, encouraged by their collective songwriting prowess, returned to Birmingham to recruit a drummer. Everett Morton (born 5 April 1951), a West Indian who had more experience – including a spell with one of Joan Armatrading's early bands – than the other three put together, took time to adapt to their punky inclinations, but proved to be a real find.

February 1979 saw the four-piece Beat play their first gigs, and acquire the services of Ranking Roger (born 21 February 1961), a black punk with dyed orange hair who drummed with a local band, the Dum Dum Boys. His extrovert character won him a frontman's role alongside Wakeling. The band's line-up was completed by the near-legendary Jamaican saxophone-player Saxa (born around 1931); while many 2-Tone bands were playing Prince Buster covers, few could claim to include one of his former sidemen in their line-up.

The Selecter offered the Beat a chance to break out of the Birmingham pubs by booking them for support gigs. They went into the studio at the end of 1979 to record a single on the 2-Tone label. The choice was the Miracles' Motown classic 'Tears Of A Clown' with Wakeling on main vocals, backed by a breakneck original, 'Rankin' Full Stop', featuring the eponymous Roger.

Like Madness, who signed a lucrative deal with Stiff after a 2-Tone hit single, the Beat stopped to assess their options after their first chart success. They decided to set up their own custom label, Go-Feet, which was distributed through Arista, and released 'Hands Off . . . She's Mine'/'Twist

Above left: The Beat's unlikely appearance belied the bright, energetic dance music they purveyed. Above: The band's 'Beat Girl' logo provided a light-hearted contrast to the 2-Tone trademark.

And Crawl' in February 1980. 'Hands Off', a tongue-in-cheek poke at male chauvinism reached Number 9 in the charts. Perhaps the best single of this early period, however, completed a Top Ten hat-trick in April; combining 'Mirror In The Bathroom' with a cover of the Pioneers' bouncy 'Jackpot', it made Number 4.

The Beat goes on

The Beat's first album, fittingly entitled *I Just Can't Stop It*, was also released in April and turned out to be one of the best party records of the period; almost unremittingly uptempo, it set a punishing pace – one American dance company complained that it was 'too fast to dance to'. Of the tracks on the LP, 'Two Swords' presented a rational yet danceable argument for pacifism, while 'Stand Down Margaret' flung Prime Minister Margaret Thatcher's words back in her face: 'I see no joy, I see only sorrow/I see no chance of your bright new tomorrow'. Released as a double A-sided single with 'Best Friend', it was a Number 22 hit, with royalties of some £15,000 being donated to the Anti Nuclear Campaign.

The LP was characterised by the urgent, chattering guitar interplay between Wakeling and Cox. Wakeling's upside-down guitar (a stance mistakenly copied from the left-handed Paul McCartney) made his downstroke Cox's upstroke, creating a pop propulsion which was emphasised by Everett Morton's reggae rhythms. Above all this floated Saxa's ethereal, echo-laden saxophone improvisations. These had become the Beat's trademark and featured strongly on December's chart entry, 'Too Nice To Talk To', which reached Number 7.

Meet the Beat

The simmering rhythms that had made the first album such a delight, however, had settled into a reggae pulse by the time of 1981's *Wha'appen*, at the expense of the original excitement. Reggae singer Cedric Myton of the Congos (a reissue of whose exquisitely laid-back *Heart Of The Congos* album in 1981 was one of the few non-Beat recordings to surface on Go-Feet) lent vocal support. The most successful tracks were the loping lovers' rock of 'Doors To Your Heart' (a Number 33 hit single), and the anti-war song 'I Am Your Flag'.

The recognition that *Wha'appen* was a musical cul-de-sac was followed in April 1982 by Saxa's retirement from live work for health reasons. The loss of such a charismatic figure was minimised, in musical terms at least, by the recruitment of Wesley Magoogan, a seasoned session man who had made his name with Hazel O'Connor. In the interim, another single,

'Hit It', had been released, but flopped when radio programmers discovered its risqué subject matter, masturbation.

On the face of it, the Beat's third LP, *Special Beat Service* (1982), was ideal for the American market. Devoid of political sloganeering, yet full of classic pop songs with strong hooks, the album – backed by constant touring – was a great success. Yet British Beat fans found it hard to relate to keyboards – played by roadie Dave Blockhead – taking the place of the chiming rhythm guitars on 'I Confess' or the sudden appearance of an accordion on 'Jeanette'.

Their lengthy US tours, however, lost the Beat much of their status in the UK. Arista, who had signed the band for the UK only, could see their returns diminishing still further, and dropped them. As a final gesture, the label released the Beat's idiosyncratic cover of Andy Williams' 'Can't Get Used To Losing You' (a track

from the first album), as a single, which became a surprise Number 3 hit. But after two appearances supporting David Bowie at Milton Keynes Bowl in July 1983, Ranking Roger and Dave Wakeling left to form a new group, General Public. Andy Cox and David Steele later formed the Fine Young Cannibals with soul-inspired vocalist Roland Gift. Their debut single in 1985, 'Johnny Come Home' was a mix of compulsive dance music with social comment and reached the UK Top Ten.

Perhaps the Beat's innocent enthusiasm took too many knocks in the cut-and-thrust world of rock; certainly they found the British public unwilling or unable to come to terms with their changes in musical direction. Yet they will be remembered for the ability they shared with the Jam, to put over political and social comment in a direct, unpretentious and danceable way.

MICHAEL HEATLEY

Below: Meet the Beat, from left Andy Cox, David Steele, Everett Morton and Ranking Roger, with Dave Wakeling and Saxa in the foreground.

How Madness took giant strides to stardom

FEW BANDS THAT had started out at the height of punk in 1976-77 were still around making hit records six years later. One group that did manage to stay the course was Madness, whose good-time dance music survived the changes in musical fashions with an uncanny ability to produce Top Ten hits one after the other.

The Camden invasion

Madness' stomping ground was the Camden Town area of London. All seven members were brought up around there, working-class boys whose lives had been hard at times, nothing more than ordinary at others.

In late 1976, the North London Invaders were formed by 18-year-old Mike Barson and 17-year-old Lee Thompson. Having stolen a Fats Domino LP from a second-hand record shop, they enjoyed endless sessions of playing along to the coveted album: Lee played an old, tinny sax, a 21-year-old friend, Chris Foreman, played drums *and* guitar and Mike, the only one who had any idea of how to string two chords together, played piano.

In June 1977 the North London Invaders engaged another drummer, Gary Dovey, and a bass player, Chas Smash; hour after hour was spent in Mike Barson's bedroom as he tried, with little success, to instil some sort of musical sensitivity into the band. Smash left after a row with Barson and Dovey quit after a punch-up with Thompson, but not before introducing 16-year-old Mark 'Bedders' Bedford to the band: despite his age, Bedders was a highly competent bassist.

The next individual to try to fill the drum vacancy was John Hasler, but he soon gave that up to become the band's manager and was replaced by an old friend of Bedders, Dan 'Woody' Woodgate. Then Barson overheard a young Graham 'Suggs'

ONE STEP BEYOND

McPherson singing on a bus and asked him to join the group as vocalist.

In 1978 the Invaders played their first gig at Acklam Hall, London, supporting reggae band Tribesman. They performed a few of Mike Barson's own songs and realised that they had created a new kind of sound. It was a sound born of endless hours listening to old Sixties Motown records and Jamaican bluebeat, together with a touch of lyrical silliness often attributed to the influence of Kilburn and the High Roads. That night they christened

Below: Madness put their best feet forward, from left Mike Barson, Suggs McPherson, Woody Woodgate, Chris Foreman, Chas Smash, Mark Bedford and Lee Thompson.

their music the 'Nutty Sound' and Chas Smash, in the audience, assured his place as second vocalist and chief 'nutty' dancer by leaping on stage and dancing frenetically, his head jerking from side to side as fast as his feet.

After a brief spell as Morris and the Minors, the band became Madness after a favourite Prince Buster song; but amid the doom and gloom of the post-punk music scene, there was little room on the pub circuit for a happy-go-lucky, good-time dance band, however exclusive their sound. According to Suggs, 'We were playing reggae and bluebeat, which was like old fogeys' music and everyone else was blasting out punk. But we kept on going because that was what we were into.' It

wasn't just the music and the dance that made Madness unique, though: the Nutty Boys had by this time formed a visual image to reflect the sound – this consisted of short, flat-topped haircuts and identical mohair/zoot suits, or pork pie hats, baggy blue jeans, Fred Perry T-shirts and Harrington jackets.

Double date
In early 1979 Madness got their big break. In Coventry, Jerry Dammers had also rediscovered ska and bluebeat and formed a band of 'rude boys' called the Specials. Dammers had created his own label, 2-Tone, and released 'Gangsters', a single that was taking the country by storm. Madness introduced themselves to

Dammers and were immediately asked to support his band at London's Nashville, the same night as Camden Town's Dublin Castle had finally relented and given them a gig. They played both dates.

In August 1979, Madness' debut single was released on 2-Tone. Entitled 'The Prince' (after Prince Buster), it stayed in the charts for 11 weeks, reaching Number 16 in October. Although indebted to Dammers and 2-Tone, Madness were nevertheless reluctant to be judged as part of the label and secondary to the Specials.

In October 1979 they were asked to play at the wedding reception of Dave Robinson, head of the independent Stiff label. By the end of October, they had signed to Stiff and released a second single and a debut album, both entitled 'One Step Beyond'. The single stayed in the charts for over three months, reaching the Number 7 position, while the album, produced by Clive Langer and Alan Winstanley, reached Number 2 and stayed in the Top 75 for 78 weeks altogether. The LP's cover displayed the Madness 'train' – a combination of the nutty dance and a moving train image. Their trademark for years to come, it was even recreated by the group for a television toothpaste commercial in 1982.

Matinée idols

At the beginning of November, Madness agreed to take part in the British 2-Tone tour, along with the Specials, the Selecter and the Bodysnatchers. The tour was an overwhelming financial success but provided the background to a potentially damaging situation. The Madness look and ska sound had attracted elements of Britain's skinhead movement and Madness, the only all-white group on the tour, became targets for National Front and British Movement offensives. The success of 'My Girl', which reached Number 2 in January 1980, was marred by a band of BM followers who insisted on 'seig heiling' and fighting at every gig – ideal fodder for a predatory press. Unable to cope with the situation, Madness quit the 2-Tone tour and left for the United States, issuing a statement to the press which insisted that 'there's no way any of us are fascist – we're categorically against it'.

Below: The Madness 'train' steams into action. Above right: Suitable attire for the 'Tomorrow's Just Another Day' video. Right: On stage in Paris. Below right: Suggs plays video villain in 'Shut Up'. Bottom right: The Camden invasion?

While no permanent damage had been done, Madness decided to play down the skinhead image and actively encourage their increasing younger ·audience. In February 1980 they played an unprecedented matinée gig in London, with entrance restricted to children of 16 and under. The gig sold out and marked the beginning of a trend for pop bands to follow. But the event that really ensured continuing success happened in September that year when, after the Top Ten hit 'Night Boat To Cairo', the archetypal Madness anthem was released.

Nutty tricks

'Baggy Trousers' epitomised the Madness sound *and* look with its cheeky schoolboy lyrics, fast, staccato rhythm, ska sax breaks and, even more important, its promotional video. Directed by Dave Robinson, the video's *pièce de resistance* was an airborne, sax-playing Lee Thompson, sporting a pair of ludicrously baggy trousers. There was no doubt that this helped push the record up to Number 3 in October 1980 and keep it in the charts for four months. There followed a series of promotional videos that were as important to Madness as the songs. The band's acting abilities, along with crazy themes, trick photography and no sartorial inhibitions whatsoever, gave them a video identity that was to remain unrivalled for many years.

The end of 1980 saw the release of a second album, *Absolutely*, a follow-up single, 'Embarrassment', more matinées and a sell-out charity show – all of which showed Madness retaining a friendly, carefree image. In 1981, after yet another Top Ten hit, 'The Return Of The Los Palmas 7', Dave Robinson decided to capitalise on their video success – only this time it was to be a major feature film about the first three years of the band's life (ending with the first Dublin Castle gig). The film starred Madness as themselves, featured their songs and was entitled, after one of the *Absolutely* tracks, *Take It Or Leave It*. Despite its success as an extended Madness video, a witty storyline and a fast city pace, the film flopped at the box office in October 1981; critics complained that out-of-tune rehearsals in a back bedroom did not constitute great cinema, others that the majority of Madness fans were so young that they had little interest in the band's early days.

Despite their failure to make it on celluloid, the band continued to churn out hit singles and sell out gigs just as they had always done. In April 1981 'Grey Day' reached Number 4; this weary, rather miserable song reflected a marked departure from the characteristic chummy cheerfulness, and its cynicism was echoed in the third album, *Seven*. Released in October, the album proved the band had not only improved musically beyond belief but that they were also beginning to write politically sensitive and even controversial lyrics.

In the autumn of 1981, 'Shut Up' and a cover version of Labi Siffre's hit 'It Must Be Love' both made the UK Top Ten, while the following February saw the release of 'Cardiac Arrest'. A comment on the stresses of modern-day living, the single was banned by the BBC because one of their DJ's fathers had died recently of a heart attack. The ban was eventually lifted, but it broke the run of Top Ten hits – the single peaked at Number 14.

In May 1982, however, 'House Of Fun' gave Madness their first Number 1. This coincided with a Number 1 album, the compilation *Complete Madness*, described by one national paper as an 'essential LP for people who wouldn't normally buy records' – and, since the videos were almost as popular as the records, Stiff also released a *Complete Madness* video cassette.

Unlike many of their contemporaries, Madness rose above their own fame and fortune and actually changed very little. Determined to keep the original 'nuttiness' intact, they remained in Camden Town and their music, although more proficient, was still exemplified by titles like 'Driving In My Car', a Number 4 hit released in July 1982, and 'Our House' (an ordinary semi-detached in an ordinary street) in November. The latter became the band's second UK Number 1 hit and a US hit and was taken from their album *The Rise And Fall*, released in 1982.

By 1983 Madness had established themselves as one of the widest-reaching successes of the time. They had stowed the baggy trousers and Crombie overcoats in favour of a more casual, less uniform look (Chas Smash, the original skinhead, even sported a beard) and, while their songs undoubtedly retained the dance-hall 'nutty' element, they became unafraid to express political sentiment: in April they joined UB40 in a benefit gig against the Sizewell B nuclear reactor site, and headlined a Campaign for Nuclear Disarmament rally at Brockwell Park, South London, in May.

Shortly afterwards keyboardist Mike Barson left the band and their contract with Stiff ended. Madness set up their own label Zarjazz and built the Liquidator studios. Their successful 1985 LP *Mad Not Mad* featured keyboards by Steve Nieve of the Attractions. They had their 20th consecutive Top Twenty hit with the single 'Yesterday's Men', followed by 'Uncle Sam' – a comment on America's influence over Britain.

By now, the British music press, which once had seen Madness as nothing more than a temporary respite for youngsters in a sea of punk gloom, had come to recognise the merits of the band.   SALLY PAYNE

Madness
Recommended Listening
Complete Madness (Stiff HIT-TV 1) (Includes: Embarrassment, Baggy Trousers, It Must Be Love, Night Boat To Cairo, House Of Fun, One Step Beyond); *The Rise And Fall* (Stiff SEEZ 46) (Includes: Rise And Fall, Tomorrow's (Just Another Day), Sunday Morning, Our House, New Delhi, Calling Card).

UB40: dole-queue reggae with a message

OF THE PLETHORA of energetic dance bands to emerge from the Midlands during the post-punk, 2-Tone era, only Dexys Midnight Runners and UB40 stayed the course. Of the two, UB40, with their political commitment and anonymous image, seemed the less likely to wear the mantle of pop stardom. But talent will out, and UB40 managed to sidestep the dictates of fashion and eventually achieve considerable commercial success.

Graduation day

The UB40 paradox began in late 1977 when three fellow students at Moseley Art College, Brian Travers, Jim Brown and Earl Falconer, got together with a bunch of like-minded friends and – like so many others at the time – decided that a lack of musical ability would be no deterrent to forming a band. Almost randomly, Travers decided to take up the saxophone, Brown opted for drums and Falconer the bass guitar. They were subsequently joined by their friends Ali and Robin Campbell (who chose, respectively, rhythm and lead guitar), Jimmy Lynn (keyboards), Norman Hassan (percussion) and Timi Tupe 'Yomi' Abeyomi Babyemi (percussion). Although they initially lacked instrumental ability, there was a strong musical sensibility in the band generated by the Campbell brothers, sons of British folk-singer Iain Campbell.

It took six months of fairly solid rehearsal before UB40 felt confident enough to perform publicly at the Horse and Hounds public house in King's Heath; at that time their repertoire was composed entirely of cover versions of reggae classics, like Augustus Clarke's 'Big And Small' and Bim Sherman's 'Lover's Leap'. By playing the Jamaican-based music that they loved and vaunting a percussion-heavy line-up, the group appealed strongly to the multi-racial, dance-crazy audiences of the moment. However, even before they had garnered a decent local following, UB40 underwent a personnel shuffle when the British immigration authorities decided that they wanted to send 'Yomi' back to his native Nigeria; at the same time, Jimmy Lynn was replaced by the brother of Ali Campbell's girlfriend, the admirably-named Mickey Virtue.

The name UB40 was taken from the identity card issued to recipients of unemployment benefit, and as such reflected the band's commitment to social issues – a commitment that, while unwavering, was often misinterpreted. They have undertaken loss-making tours of African countries – like Zimbabwe – that rarely see multi-racial bands, they have performed at fund-raising gigs for anarchist organisations such as the Autonomy Club, yet have publicly decried the much better-known Rock Against Racism organisation. 'RAR seems to dodge a lot of important issues,'

said Jim Brown in 1980, while Ali Campbell added '. . . the world seems to be in the middle of a wild plunge into right-wing madness. The people that we're against are violent and you can't fight them off with words. I think that's why RAR became such a nonentity.'

Items on toast

Eschewing popular causes was typical of UB40's collective morality and their staunch belief in it. Right from the start, they avoided the temptations of major record companies who were holding out 'custom label' deals to the new ska/reggae bands, like the Beat, who were assigned the Go-Feet label by Arista. Instead they signed to David Virr's Dudley-based Graduate Records for a straight 50-50 royalty split, but the consequent lack of an advance threw them into debt when they discovered that escalating popularity meant they had to buy bigger and better equipment.

Just before signing with Graduate,

UB40 were joined by Astro (real name Terence Wilson), who had been running his own reggae disco show around the Birmingham clubs where the group often played. Astro fulfilled the role of frontman, or 'toaster', in much the same way as Ranking Roger of the Beat or Chas Smash of Madness, but later went on to become a far more important part of the band's musical mosaic by learning to play trumpet and forming one third of the UB40 brass section with Travers and Hassan.

Although Astro was always the most visible member of UB40 on stage, the band practiced a fierce democracy in every other respect, sharing writing credits and royalties, refusing to appoint a single spokesman and insisting instead that the music spoke for them. Thus they became one of the most anonymous of contemporary pop bands – indeed their first three Graduate singles, together with the majority of their albums, did not carry a picture of the group on their cover.

In keeping with their provincial independence, the band used a local producer, Bob Lamb, an ex-member of Birmingham

reggae band Locomotive (who had had a UK Top Thirty hit in 1968 with 'Rudi's In Love'). Lamb's home-built studio was so small that he could only accommodate the band by recording them in shifts – but the results were highly impressive.

In 1979, the Pretenders surprised the music business by inviting UB40 to join them on their first major UK tour and, helped by this exposure, UB40's single, 'King'/'Food For Thought', entered the Top

Twenty the following March and climbed to Number 4. A follow-up single, 'My Way Of Thinking', went to Number 6 in June,

Bottom: UB40; standing from left Astro, Brian Travers, Robin Campbell, Norman Hassan, and Jim Brown; sitting from left Mickey Virtue, Earl Falconer and Ali Campbell. Below: Ali Campbell at the microphone. Below left: Robin Campbell and Astro deliver the goods.

while their debut album, *Signing Off*, reached Number 2 in September and stayed on the LP charts for a staggering 71 weeks, achieving the highest sales to date of any independent LP. In November, they notched up another Top Ten single with 'The Earth Dies Screaming'.

Labour of love

In 1981, the band decided they needed even more control of their records and left Graduate and started their own label, DEP International. They found continuing success with this new venture: the first DEP single, 'Don't Let It Pass You By', reached Number 16, while the second, 'One In Ten', made Number 7, despite the rather gloomy nature of its lyric. A new album, *Present Arms*, reached Number 2 in the LP charts in the summer, while in September the band took the bold step of releasing a dub version of the record; *Present Arms In Dub* underlined UB40's commitment to roots music and, despite its parochial appeal, made the LP Top Forty.

By the end of 1981, however, the public's appetite for Anglicised reggae and ska was wearing thin, the Selecter and the Specials had broken up and UB40's next three singles barely dented the Top Thirty. The following year found the band moving discreetly away from their fairly strict reggae posture, harnessing more melodic tunes and romantic lyrics to a softer beat.

In 1983, however, there was a pronounced UB40 revival, doubtless a result of the band's musical maturity. They finally reached a Number 1 single with the lilting, hugely catchy 'Red Red Wine' – a cover of the old Neil Diamond song first played reggae-style by Tony Tribe – and topped the album charts with *Labour Of Love*, a collection of cover versions of early-Seventies reggae songs that paid tribute to their influences.

The band's 1985 LP *Baggaridim* featured mainly old UB40 numbers 'toasted' over by Birmingham reggae artists. UB40 were also aiming their sights at the US market. They toured the US several times and the single 'I Got You Babe' with Pretenders Chrissie Hynde on vocals was a hit in the US as well as making Number 1 in the UK.

Finally the years of operating in their own, uncompromising fashion had paid off: UB40 had established themselves unequivocally as a musical co-operative of enduring quality. As Jim Brown said back in 1980: 'Some people will say that, first and foremost, we're a dance band, but I really think we've got a responsibility which overrides being a dance band. A dance band is a package to sell your politics.'

'Wine' topped the US charts in 1988, while another cover, Sonny and Cher's 'I Got You Babe', made the top in the UK in 1985. Despite four more LPs of original material, UB40 found most success with the songs of others. ALASTAIR DOUGALL

REGGAE UK

Black sounds from Britain's inner cities

FOR THE BLACK community in the UK in the Fifties, the 'house blues' party was the mainstay of the weekend's entertainment – a cultural refuge in the midst of an often hostile host community. Everyone came together – Jamaican, Trinidadian, St Lucian – and rocked their troubles away to the sounds of Fats Domino, Bobby 'Blue' Bland, Johnny Ace or Amos Milburn. Rhythm and blues was the staple musical diet of the first sound-system operators like Duke Vin or Count Suckle, but as the Sixties approached, the new music of Jamaica became the dominant musical force.

The ascendancy of the ska beat coincided with Jamaica's independence in 1962, and up-and-coming young acts like Jimmy Cliff and Toots and the Maytals proved stiff competition for the old-established blues and boogie singers like Laurel Aitken. Aitken decided to emigrate to England, and soon established himself as the house producer of the Blue Beat label. The first generation of JA/UK session players followed, including veteran trombonist Rico Rodriguez, who had left the Skatalites and decided to make England his home, along with saxophonist Joe Harriot and others.

Musical monopoly

Ska merged into rocksteady and rocksteady into reggae. The music press was unanimous in their declaration that reggae, a music associated in the UK with the skinhead cult, was cheap and inferior compared with soul. Despite such critical disdain, a Methodist youth club in the North London suburb of Harlesden saw the birth of the Cimarons in 1967. At that time the only black bands working the UK live circuit were both soul bands, Jimmy James and the Vagabonds and Geno Washington and the Ram Jam Band. With the reggae market to themselves, the Cimarons set about backing virtually every Jamaican singer to tour or record in the UK between 1968 and 1972.

A visit to Africa by the group in the midst of the Nigerian civil war led to a radical shift in consciousness. By 1974, the Cimarons were overtly Rastafarian in outlook, had recorded their *On The Rocks* album in Jamaica and topped the charts there for seven consecutive weeks with their version of Bob Marley's 'Talking Blues'. The mid Seventies was a critical period for the Cimarons, who headed a new wave of young roots reggae musicians whose enthusiasm for live performance signalled an alternative to the sound-system circuit.

In Jamaica in 1976, reggae was a melting-pot of radical politics and apocalyptic Rastafarian imagery set to a militant rockers beat. Its main ambassador, Bob Marley, was conquering the world with his *Natty Dread* album and a stage show unprecedented in reggae; the Wailers were as tight and heavy on stage as in the studio, and were a serious inspiration to any aspiring young musician who saw

them. Record companies were falling over themselves to sign reggae artists and the music press was littered with features from Jamaica.

It was the summer of 1976 that was to prove most critical. Punk made the headlines, and the adoption of reggae by bands such as the Clash and the Slits saw punk and reggae bands come together in unity. Rock Against Racism was instrumental in opening up a vast new audience for UK reggae clubs and pubs.

In the depths of London's Ladbroke Grove, the Metro Youth Club was the local hub of activity. One regular was a young bass player, George Oban, who had returned after a spell in Jamaica with the intention of forming a band. Together with Brinsley Forde, he recruited 15-year-old drummer Angus Gaye from the Metronome Steel Band, guitarist Donald Griffiths and Courtney Hemmings on keyboards. Their first album, *Aswad*, was released in 1976 to critical acclaim, yet they were confronted with a consistently hostile audience on their first major tour as support for pub-rockers turned punks Eddie and the Hot Rods. But the climate was changing with the help of Don Letts, the DJ at London's premier punk venue, the Roxy where punk and reggae enjoyed a close and fruitful relationship.

Aswad recorded with and backed Jamaican legend Burning Spear on his first UK tour in 1977, yet despite extensive touring in their own right and appearances at the numerous Rock Against Racism concerts, their recorded output was erratic. Frustration led to a clash over musical direction and George Oban was dropped from the band. Brinsley's acting and Aswad's musical role in the film *Babylon* (1980) further enhanced their reputation.

Misty in Roots came together in Southall, West London, where they formed their own People Unite collective. Their hypnotic songs of redemption owned more to Burning Spear than Bob Marley, and they were arguably the most uncompromising and least commercial of all the youth bands. BBC Radio One DJ John Peel voted their *Live At The Counter Eurovision '79* his album of the year. Another London band to break through in the late Seven-

ties were Black Slate, who scored a UK Number 9 hit in 1980 with the catchy 'Amigo'. Although they failed to score further pop successes on this scale, their musicians featured on many other notable UK productions.

Steel Pulse brought theatrics, compelling harmonies and razor-edged lyrics from Birmingham to London's Vortex and Hope and Anchor in 1977. Their wide exposure to white audiences on the circuit undoubtedly helped push their first album, 1978's *Handsworth Revolution*, to Number 9 in the album charts. After the sacking of lead singer Michael Riley, however, the group began to pursue a commitment to Rastafari and moved away from the more immediate issues of the day – a move that hit sales of the excellent *Tribute To The Martyrs* (1979) and subsequent albums. Two Bristol bands, Black Roots and Talisman, were also prominent on the gig circuit.

For lovers only

The other side of the UK reggae coin was lovers' rock. Sound systems still provided the main sources of musical entertinment in the black community, and lovers' rock was strictly studio music made for the party or the dancehall. The first lovers' rock tune was 'Caught You In A Lie', sung by Louisa Mark, played by Matumbi and produced by sound system operator Lloyd Coxsone in 1979.

Key roles in the development of this softer side of the music were played by Matumbi and, in particular, their guitarist Dennis Bovell. Formed in 1971, Matumbi pioneered that mellow fusion of soul and reggae which characterised the lovers' rock genre. By the late Seventies, producers like Castro Brown, Winston Edwards and Bovell had launched numerous sweet, sugary girl vocal groups. Although artists like Jean Adebambo and Carrol Thompson remained cult names, one-off pop successes like Janet Kay's 'Silly Games' (a Number 2 pop hit in 1979) or Sugar Minott's 'Good Thing Going' (a Number 4 in 1981) proved the size of lovers' rock's potential audience.

The lack of direction that was reflected in early Eighties pop music generally was equally evident among the ranks of UK reggae performers. Even the once-proud Cimarons had been reduced to recording an album of Paul McCartney's pop hits in reggae style in a bid for chart success.

It was fitting, then, that Aswad should top the UK charts in 1988 with 'Don't Turn Around'. Even Cliff Richard was keen to record with a band which had finally arrived.

PAUL BRADSHAW

Top right: Aswad, the young lions of UK reggae, prowl their Ladbroke Grove neighbourhood. Far right: The seven-piece Steel Pulse line-up that cut 1978's Handsworth Revolution *album. Above right: Pulse in rehearsal. Right: The pioneering Cimarons on stage during their Rasta-influenced Seventies phase.*

Keeping up the pace with Dexys Midnight Runners

DEXYS MIDNIGHT RUNNERS first became known to the public when they appeared third on the bill to the Specials and the Selecter half-way through the 2-Tone package tour of Britain in the winter of 1979. Dexys later rejected their association with 2-Tone, although they did have a certain affiliation with the movement. Like the 2-Tone bands, they came from the Midlands (Birmingham) and they also played Sixties-influenced music, although their inspiration was not bluebeat and ska but soul. Their influences included both American artists on the Atlantic and Motown labels and British acts like Cliff Bennett and the Rebel Rousers and, especially, Geno Washington and the Ram Jam Band. At the end of the tour, Dexys severed their 2-Tone links; they did not sign with the label but released their first single, 'Dance Stance', on ex-Clash manager Bernie Rhodes' Oddball Records, taking on Rhodes' associate, Dave Corke, as manager.

Off to a flying start

Dexys Midnight Runners were formed by singer/guitarists Kevin Rowland and Al Archer after their previous group, the Killjoys, had disbanded in 1977. Rowland and Archer decided to use what skill they had acquired from this initial venture to form a group playing the music they loved. It took a while for them to assemble a stable line-up, but by the time Dexys played the 2-Tone tour and recorded 'Dance Stance', Rowland and Archer had been joined by Pete Williams (bass, vocals), Pete Saunders (organ, piano), Bobby Junior (drums), Big Jim Paterson (trombone), Steve Spooner (alto sax) and tenor-sax player Jeff 'J.B.' Blythe, a highly accomplished and experienced musician and veteran of Geno Washington's Ram Jam Band. He was responsible for Dexys' distinctive brass arrangements such as the rousing intro of 'Dance Stance', a fine single that unaccountably failed to chart.

Rowland's vocal on the record was rather low-key, but by the time Dexys had signed with EMI and headlined their own Intense Emotion Revue tour in 1980, he and Archer had perfected a more dynamic and expressive style of taut, clipped consonants and slurred, choked vowels that were as melismatic as Sixties black soul singers but bore little or no trace of an American accent. The black singing style it most closely resembled was that of Chairman of the Board frontman General Johnson, whose 'Brrrr' vocal mannerism was employed to great effect by Rowland on Dexys' second single 'Geno'.

Dexys' novel approach extended beyond their music to include the 'working-class' dress of donkey-jackets, plimsolls and woolly hats worn by several of the band and their uncompromising attitude to their audiences. Both these aspects were

Celtic Soul

symptomatic of a determination to avoid the mannered approach of other British 'soul revival' acts and to create a modern, honest music that would rival in intensity that of the great soul artists of the Sixties.

'Geno' (a tribute to Geno Washington) hit the UK Number 1 spot just as the group, which now included Andy 'Stoker' Growcott (drums) and Andde Leek (keyboards), began its tour. Confronted by capacity audiences clamouring to hear 'Geno', Dexys insisted that the fans should take the rest of their show seriously, quickly gaining themselves a reputation for cantankerous behaviour.

Rowland implored the crowd to calm down and search for their 'inner soul', while the total silence required for the whispered intro to 'I'm Just Looking' was often obtained by Rowland, Archer, Spooner, Blythe, Williams and Paterson lining up at the front of the stage to stare down any hecklers. Dexys demanded the same degree of commitment to the music

Left: Kevin Rowland, architect of Dexys Midnight Runners' Eighties success. Below: The band's original line-up, featuring guitarist Al Archer (second from left). Below right: Keeping the fans at bay.

on the part of their fans as they gave themselves. This commitment was reflected by the group's frugal lifestyle on the road.

Out of breath

In July 1980, following a series of acrimonious press interviews, Dexys issued a statement in the music papers to the effect that henceforth their views would be published only in the form of their own 'essays'. This extraordinary move coincided with rumours that the group had hijacked the master tapes of their first LP, *Searching For The Young Soul Rebels* (1980), and were holding them while they argued with EMI about the terms of their contract. When they had resolved their difficulties with EMI, the album was released to ecstatic reviews. The ballad 'I Couldn't Help If I Tried' featured a particularly inspired vocal performance by Rowland, while 'There There My Dear' was a ferocious, brass-laden tirade against blindly following fashion. It later made Number 7 in the singles charts.

The album's killer punch, however, was 'Keep It', on which the horns simmered and then boiled over behind Archer's contemptuous vocal. The album also heralded the return of Saunders, following the

departure of Andde Leek. After another British tour, Saunders left for good; he was replaced by Mick Talbot, formerly of South London group the Merton Parkas.

After returning from some successful dates in the US, Dexys went into hiding amid rumours that they had split up. In October, it was announced that Blythe, Spooner, Williams, Growcott and Talbot had left following a disagreement during a recording of the band's fourth single, 'Keep It Part II'. This turned out to be a re-recording of the album track with Rowland and Archer hysterically singing new lyrics that indicated the group's doubtful future.

The single flopped, and silence fell until the spring of 1981 when the departed members launched their new outfit, the Bureau, with singer Archie Brown, guitarist Rob Jones and trombonist Paul Taylor. The Bureau's shows were in the tradition of Dexys' early gigs and the band stressed their determination to retain the passion and integrity of their former outfit. Sadly, after the commercial failure of two singles and an album, the Bureau disbanded. Talbot later joined ex-Jam leader Paul Weller in the Style Council.

Meanwhile, Rowland, Archer and Paterson had recruited former Secret Affair

drummer Seb Shelton, keyboardist Micky Billingham, bassist Steve Wynne and sax-players Brian Maurice (alto) and Paul Speare (tenor). Before this new line-up could take the stage, however, Al Archer elected to strike out on his own and was replaced by guitarist Billy Adams.

Dexys' comeback single 'Plan B' was a glorious rush of sound kicked off by Rowlands' firm testament 'You've always been searching for something' and carried by a tri-umphant solo from Paterson, who had taken over from Archer and Blythe as Rowland's co-writer and the group's brass arranger. Over the next few months, the band gave sporadic perform-ances of their Projected Passion Revue, immaculately turned out in hooded track-suits, boxing boots and short pony-tails.

Emerald Express

The Projected Passion Revue also featured comedians, a dance troupe and, in the later shows, Paterson, Speare and Maurice on celli and viola. This string section was first heard on record on 'Liars A To E', the un-successful follow-up to the Number 16 hit 'Show Me'. Instead of mirroring the shim-mering evanescence of the Philadelphia sound, the strings sounded more like a classical quartet. This intimate feel be-came a crucial part of Dexys' sound on the next single, 'The Celtic Soul Brothers', which saw Wynne replaced by Giorgio Kilkenny and the incorporation of fiddlers Steve Brennan and Helen O'Hara.

Dexys' follow-up, 'Come On Eileen', brought the band their second UK Number 1 and featured brass alongside the strings of the Emerald Express. The resulting sound, superbly realised on the ballad 'Old' on the LP *Too Rye Ay* (1982) – was similar to, though slightly rougher than – the blend of Irish folk, soul and R&B pioneered by Van Morrison since *St Dominic's Pre-view* (1972). Dexys acknowledged their debt to Morrison by covering his 'Jackie Wilson Said' on *Too Rye Ay*; it later made Number 5 in the UK singles charts, while 'Come On Eileen' entered the US charts to provide Dexys with their first US hit single.

To match the change in Dexys' music, the band used a different image to promote the LP, kitting themselves out like gypsies with tangled hair and torn dungarees.

After working on the album, Paterson left the band. He was followed by Speare and Maurice, who joined him in the TKO Horns, a freelance brass team. Dexys thenceforth employed hired musicians to support the group's nucleus.

By 1985 Dexys image had changed yet again – this time to the slick and smoothed-back hair of so many of the early Eighties bands. Their LP *Don't Stand Me Down* continued to explore Rowland's favourite themes, and provided the single '(An Extract From) This Is What She's Like' in November 1985, marking the start of their UK tour entitled 'The Dexys Mid-night Runners Coming To Town Tour'.

Dexys' early-Eighties 'sporty' image (top) preceded their Romany look (above) which lasted until 1985.

Rowland then disbanded Dexys, opting for a solo career. His first album, *The Wan-derer,* was released in 1988 but was nowhere near as successful as his former group.   JOHN VOYSEY

Men of Metal

How the new wave of HM filled the power vacuum in Eighties rock

IF, AS MUDDY WATERS' song title put it, 'The blues had a baby and they named it rock'n'roll', then it should be pointed out that rock'n'roll was not slow in sowing a few wild oats of its own. Somewhere along the line it produced a hulking, bawling brat called heavy metal, which it left, dumped and disowned, on the doorstep of the Eighties.

The roots of heavy metal go all the way back to the Sixties, although its exact beginnings are shrouded in the mists of many a dry ice machine. It could be argued that the 1969 Woodstock Festival, featuring such acts as Janis Joplin, Ten Years After, Mountain, the Who and Johnny Winter, marked the beginning of a new era of ever-bigger bands playing to ever-larger audiences at ever-louder volumes. An earlier landmark was Led Zeppelin's first album, released in 1968, but most commentators refer back even further to the dawn of the heavy electric guitar bands at the end of 1966, when Cream released their debut album *Fresh Cream* and the Jimi Hendrix Experience's first single, 'Hey Joe', was in the shops just too late for Christmas. Perhaps it all started as early as 1964 when the Kinks discovered the first *bona fide* power-chord riff on 'You Really Got Me', added a raucous vocal and freak-out guitar solo and steered

the record to the Number 1 position in the UK charts.

Whatever the precise starting point, heavy metal has endured almost as long as rock itself, although it has not always answered to its present name. But whereas rock, and modern popular music generally, expanded and developed to take on board a huge variety of new influences, plundering many different ethnic and technological sources in its restless search for inspiration, heavy metal sustained itself in a state of almost totally arrested development. Admittedly, the standard of playing improved over the years, while the amount of equipment increased dramatically as volume escalated; some heavy-metal bands even introduced keyboards, although the keyboard player was obliged, when required, to produce a sound resembling a small atom bomb exploding on the auditorium roof.

Heavy metal is escapism pure and simple, and this may explain why it is so beloved of its fans and universally condemned by the critical élite. The frequently violent imagery, such as that portrayed by Iron Maiden's album-cover

Motorhead and Twisted Sister indulge in a bludgeoning axe jam. The strutting, posturing guitar hero remained at the centre of heavy metal into the Eighties.

and promotional graphics, has provided persuasive ammunition for the music's detractors; but the violence has largely been confined to the images, and paradoxically heavy-metal audiences have boasted an enviable reputation for good behaviour. Sexist lyrics, abundantly and crassly exemplified by David Coverdale's Whitesnake, are another cross that the genre has had to bear, although the threat has again proved worse than the reality; this was primarily the stuff of adolescent fantasy – for boys who, in the main, are polite to their mums.

Heavy metal suffered something of a lean period in the mid-Seventies. Led Zeppelin, Deep Purple and Black Sabbath had become international superstars beyond approach, leaving a distinct gap in the market for bands willing to play at grass-roots venues. The press, by and large, ignored or scorned the groups that were around. One notable exception was *Sounds*, who continued their favourable coverage and whose editor Geoff Barton, along with DJ Tommy Vance, became a media champion of the cause.

Onslaught of the axemen

The turn of the Eighties, however, saw a renewed upsurge of groups who were dubbed the 'new wave' of British heavy metal by *Sounds*. It heralded a worldwide renaissance of the genre: AC/DC from Australia, Rush from Canada and Van Halen in America joined such new British groups as Iron Maiden, Def Leppard, Saxon, and Motorhead in the charts. In the UK, *Sounds'* publishers Spotlight capitalised on the staff's enthusiasm and expertise by launching the fanzine-style *Guitar Heroes* ('snaps of long-haired chaps leaning over backwards in colour', commented the *Rock Yearbook IV*) and the successful *Kerrang!*.

Although heavy metal had a massive and loyal army of fans that allowed it to thrive when most of the music industry was in a recession, it remained a closed world within the larger music scene. Although its sound and values stemmed from the most basic rock'n'roll traditions, the whole bludgeoning, overblown

heavy-metal circus alienated all but the most committed of fans.

Heavy metal has never been afraid to build on its past. New young fans still delve reverently into their older brothers' Hendrix collections, and new players pay heed to the techniques and skills of their forebears. This infusion of new blood and fresh enthusiasm has secured heavy metal's niche in the popular music scene of the Eighties.　　DAVID SINCLAIR

Opposite: Swiss band Krokus pose before a typical HM-style backdrop. Above: An invisible guitar player duels with the real thing. Below: Saxon uphold another enduring HM image as leather-clad bikers.

ROCK '79

1979 saw Mods back on the streets of Britain in their parka jackets riding scooters, allowing bands like the Merton Parkas and Secret Affair a few brief months of glory. The Who, survivors of the original Mod era, played their first gig since drummer Keith Moon's death and *Quadrophenia,* the film which captured those days, was released.

Multi-racial Coventry band the Specials set up their own 2-Tone label whose artists included Madness, Selecter and the Beat. The 2-Tone gigs and tours, however, were frequently marred by what was thought to be political aggression, involving the National Front and the British Movement. Still plagued by violence at their gigs, Sham 69 finally split up, as did many of the first-generation punk bands, while the death of Sex Pistol Sid Vicious gave punk its only candidate for martyrdom.

The UK continued to produce some exciting new-wave acts, among which were the Skids, the Members, the Ruts, the Undertones and XTC. 1979 also saw two blonde bombshells attain superstar status in Debbie Harry of Blondie and Sting of the Police, while Bowie imitator Gary Numan emerged as the nation's brightest hope.

In the US, adult-oriented rock continued to rule the airwaves in the shape of bands such as Journey, Toto and the Pointer Sisters, while the disco beat surged on with the music of Amii Stewart, Anita Ward, Sister Sledge and Chic. Despite the competition, rock veterans like the Eagles, James Taylor, Neil Young and Eric Clapton still made assaults on the charts.

January

1 The Grateful Dead top the bill on the closing night of San Francisco's Winterland.
5 Jazz bass-player Charles Mingus dies of a heart attack in Mexico.
9 A benefit concert for UNICEF is held in New York. Called a Gift of Song, it features Linda Ronstadt, the Bee Gees, Olivia Newton-John and more. Each song is donated without restriction to UNICEF.

February

2 Sid Vicious dies of a heroin overdose in New York.

Below left: Punk poet John Cooper Clarke toured the UK in June. Below: Little Feat's Lowell George died the same month.

16 Elvis Costello and the Attractions play the Palomino Club in Los Angeles. His set includes three numbers by country star Jim Reeves.
17 The Clash start their debut US tour under the banner Pearl Harbor '79. The first night is at the New York Palladium.
23 Dire Straits start their US tour.
24 Punk group Generation X are forced off stage at Barbarella's in Birmingham, after only 20 minutes as they are pelted with cans and glasses.

March

8 Johnny Rotten walks out of the film preview of *The Great Rock'n'Roll Swindle* in London's Wardour Street after members of his current group Public Image Ltd are turned away at the door.
16 Elvis Costello is involved in a brawl in the Holiday Inn in Columbus, Ohio. While drinking in the bar with Bonnie Bramlett and Stephen Stills, Costello reportedly made racist remarks about Ray Charles and James Brown, and Bramlett hit him.

April

14 Bob Dylan chooses Dire Straits' Mark Knopfler and Pick Withers to back him on his new album.
17 Wayne County releases his album *Things Your Mother Never Told You,* supposedly packaged in the first ever washable LP sleeve.
22 Keith Richard plays two charity concerts for the blind which he had been ordered to do by a Toronto judge after a Canadian heroin conviction in the previous year.

Irish band The Undertones have a UK Top Twenty hit with 'Jimmy Jimmy'.

May

1 Sales of the Bee Gees' *Saturday Night Fever* double album reach 25 million.
2 The Who play their first concert since the death of drummer Keith Moon at London's Rainbow Theatre with ex-Faces member Kenney Jones as Moon's replacement.
5 Ex-Marbles singer Graham Bonnett joins heavy-metal band Rainbow.
19 Gary Numan's group Tubeway Army top the UK charts with the electronic 'Are "Friends" Electric'.
27 Wayne County is ordered to pay £50 compensation to a 15-year-old girl fan he pleaded guilty to assaulting after a can-throwing incident at London's Lyceum.

June

1 Punk poet John Cooper Clarke kicks off his first headlining tour of the UK at Sussex University.
2 Blondie's 'Sunday Girl' is Number 1 in the UK.
7 David Bowie and Bette Midler are

seen dining out together at the Cafe Un Deux Trois in New York.
Showaddywaddy become the first Western group to be televised by satellite to Cuba.
16 The Ruts' 'Babylon's Burning' reaches Number 7 in the UK singles charts.
29 Lowell George, founder member of Little Feat, dies of a heart attack after a solo concert in Washington DC.
30 Johnny Rotten and Joan Collins appear on the panel of the revived BBC-TV show 'Juke Box Jury', hosted by Noel Edmunds.

July
1 The Electric Light Orchestra announce their intention to send a hot air balloon around the UK that summer instead of doing a tour.
13 Chuck Berry is jailed for four months by a Los Angeles court for tax evasion, and ordered to do 1000 hours of community service.
21 Thin Lizzy sack guitarist Gary Moore after he fails to appear for two gigs during their US tour. Ex Slik and Rich Kids guitarist Midge Ure flies in as his temporary replacement.
The Tom Robinson Band split up.

August
11 Jimmy Pursey signs a solo recording deal with Polydor Records.
18 Singer/songwriter/producer Nick Lowe marries country singer Carlene Carter in Los Angeles.
25 The Boomtown Rats' single 'I Don't Like Mondays' runs into a legal storm in the US. The lawyer defending Brenda Spencer, whose shooting of schoolmates inspired the song, claims it could prejudice her trial.

September
1 Cliff Richard has his first Number 1 in the UK for 14 years with the single 'We Don't Talk Anymore'.
7 Siouxsie and the Banshees' tour grinds to a halt when guitarist John McKay and drummer Kenny Morris leave the band after a disagreement.
22 XTC have a UK Top Twenty hit with 'Making Plans For Nigel'.
28 Jimmy McCulloch, former guitarist with Thunderclap Newman, Stone the Crows and Wings, is found dead in his North London flat.

October
6 The Police make Number 1 in the UK charts with 'Message In A Bottle'.
19 The Nashville in London bans skinhead-type bands after violence at an Angelic Upstarts gig.
20 Bob Dylan appears on 'Saturday Night Live' where he reveals he is a born-again Christian. He performs his gospel-influenced number 'Gotta Serve Somebody'.

November
18 Bob Dylan gives the first of four benefit concerts at the Santa Monica Civic,

Above: Irish combo the Undertones hit the British Top Twenty in April with 'Jimmy Jimmy'. Below: Folk group Fiddlers Dram had a singalong Christmas Top Tenner with 'Day Trip To Bangor (Didn't We Have A Lovely Time)'. The band never appeared in the charts again. Bottom: Mod revivalists Secret Affair.

Los Angeles. The proceeds go to World Vision, an international Christian relief organisation.
24 The Jam are Number 1 in the UK with 'Eton Rifles', while Styx top the US charts with 'Babe'.

December
1 The Human League are dropped as support on the Talking Heads' UK tour after they announce their intention to play pre-recorded tapes, show slides and watch from the audience.
4 In a rush to get to the best seats, 11 people are trampled to death at a Who concert in Cincinnati, Ohio.
15 Fiddler's Dram, a folk group from Kent, reach Number 3 in the UK charts with their single 'Day to Trip To Bangor'. Pink Floyd have their first ever UK Number 1 single with 'Another Brick In The Wall Part Two'.
26 Four nights of benefit gigs for Kampuchea begins at London's Hammersmith Odeon. Performers include Queen, Ian Dury, the Clash, the Who, the Pretenders, the Specials and Wings.
29 Blondie are confirmed as the best-selling act of the year in the UK with their LP *Parallel Lines*.

ANNETTE KENNERLEY, JENNY DAWSON

HIGH Voltage

The positive charge of AC/DC

FROM THE OUTSET, AC/DC threatened to turn the rock world upside-down with their rib-crushing, bloodcurdling brand of rock. During the first 10 years of their existence, the group led a renaissance of power rock, inspiring a host of imitators and selling more than 25 million albums in the process. But although AC/DC were the leaders of the mid-Seventies new wave of heavy metal, their hard-rock sound borrowed more from the blues tradition of Chuck Berry and Bo Diddley than it did from Deep Purple or Black Sabbath. The band dealt exclusively in power, but mercifully eschewed the HM cliches of sword-and-sorcery and exaggerated stage poses. A sense of humour, so lacking in other HM outfits, was the very essence of AC/DC's motivation and *modus operandi*.

AC/DC aimed their music below the navel and above the knees, cataloguing the concerns and interests of their vast audience through such vulgar anthems as 'Big Balls', 'Let Me Put My Love Into You' and 'Let's Get It Up'. But lyrics and titles were a mere obligation, an adjunct to the primary business at hand: AC/DC were a classic guitar band, who rapidly mastered a style that left little room for subtlety. And although, initially at least, the rock press seemed to despise the band – 'AC/DC is an Australian hard-rock band whose main purpose on earth apparently is to offend anyone within sight or earshot. They succeed on both counts', commented *Rolling Stone* – an ever-growing army of loyal fans felt very differently.

Dirty deeds

AC/DC were formed by Angus and Malcolm Young, the youngest of seven brothers born in Glasgow. In the Fifties, older sister Margaret introduced the boys to the harsher strains of American rock-'n'roll; the brothers all developed strong musical inclinations and four of them would take up music professionally. The first was Alex, who left home in the early Sixties to play bass with Tony Sheridan's Big Six and, later, Emile Ford's Checkmates; he subsequently changed his name to George Alexander, joined Grapefruit (who had a UK Number 21 hit in 1968 with 'Dear Delilah') and signed to Apple Publishing as a songwriter.

The next brother to enter the pop world was George, who formed the Easybeats in Australia in 1963, after the Young family had emigrated. The group notched up eight consecutive Top Ten hits down under be-

fore venturing to London where George and partner Harry Vanda wrote the power-pop classic 'Friday On My Mind', an international hit in 1966.

With their two older brothers finding success as rock musicians, Angus and Malcolm never considered any other careers for a moment. After serving time with a number of unrecorded outfits around Sydney, the two guitar-playing brothers formed AC/DC in 1973. After a number of line-up changes that year, they finally settled on drummer Phil Rudd, bassist Mark Evans and singer Bon Scott, the latter formerly of Australian pop acts the Valentines and Fraternity. Responsibility for AC/DC's production and career guidance was handed to Harry Vanda and George Young.

The band's first album, *High Voltage*, emerged in 1975 and was an immediate success in Australia, a country with a proud tradition of ballsy boogie bands. The LP stayed on the Australian charts for six months, selling more than 100,000 copies, and the group proved equally successful with singles, hitting the country's Top Ten with 'It's A Long Way To The Top (If You Wanna Rock'n'Roll)', 'TNT', 'Jailbreak' and 'Baby Please Don't Go' in rapid succession. Following another Australian hit album, *Dirty Deeds Done Dirt Cheap*, the group departed for London in April 1976, determined to break into the international rock market.

Ignored or ridiculed by the rock press at the height of the initial punk boom, AC/DC set about winning a British audience on their own terms – and, within a year of

their arrival, they were headlining at the Hammersmith Odeon. Gradually the press changed its tune, swayed by the band's power and lack of pretension and the charisma of the salacious but lovable Bon Scott and the frantically energetic Angus Young. On stage, Angus was very much the focal point, bouncing around manically, dressed in schoolboy's shorts, cap and tie. *Sounds*' Dave Lewis enthused over the guitarist's 'frenzied schoolboy lunacy as he traverses the stage, making Chuck Berry's duck-walk look like a paraplegic's hobble, and oozing sweat, snot and slime like some grotesque human sponge being savagely squeezed by the intensity of his own guitar playing'. In AC/DC's early days, Young had been a brash, exuberant axe-basher, by the end of 1976, he had matured into a clean, precise player with a blues style all his own.

In 1977, the group returned to Australia to work on a new album at Sydney's Albert Studios. *Let There Be Rock*, released in October, provided AC/DC with their first international success, reaching Number 17 in the UK charts and selling healthily throughout Europe. *Powerage*, issued the following May, fared equally well, but it was not until October's *If You Want Blood You've Got It* that the group succeeded in capturing their true power on record for the first time. Recorded live at dates on three continents, the LP finally conveyed a hint of the awesome intensity of the band in their natural surroundings – concert halls.

Despite the strength of the album, it made little impression in the US, being considered too rough and raucous for radio airplay. The band's record company, Atlantic, was keen to break AC/DC in the States and put pressure on the group to drop Vanda and Young as producers. Reluctantly, they agreed and, after abortive sessions with Atlantic staff producer Eddie Kramer, recorded a new album in England with Robert John 'Mutt' Lange.

Lange was by no means the equal of Vanda and Young in terms of tempestuous rock production, but he did have an excellent understanding of the dictates of US radio. Without sacrificing any of the power, he smoothed out AC/DC's rough edges on *Highway To Hell*, and the result was a US hit album. It went on to sell more than three and a half million copies worldwide and established AC/DC as one of the world's most popular hard-rock bands.

On 18 February 1980, tragedy struck when Bon Scott was found dead in a car in London following one of his regular drinking bouts. Despite his rowdy, macho-man image, Scott had been a softly-spoken, genial man and his loss was a bitter blow to the group. AC/DC were determined to carry on, however, and quickly recruited a new vocalist in Brian Johnson, whose former band Geordie had scored a handful of pop hits in the early Seventies.

A new album, *Back In Black*, released in

Opposite: A sweat-drenched Angus Young bares his chest and boogies. Inset left: AC/DC up against the wall in 1976, from left Phil Rudd, Mark Evans, Angus Young, Malcolm Young and Bon Scott. Above right: Scott smiles in the locker room.

July, proved to be the band's most fully-realised record thus far. It topped the LP charts in the US, UK and Australia, and by the end of the year had sold over 10 million worldwide. The band had become so popular in the US that a belated issue of *Dirty Deeds Done Dirt Cheap*, recorded five years previously, made Number 1, while 'You Shook Me All Night Long', a single taken from *Back In Black*, made the Top Forty on both sides of the Atlantic.

A hugely successful world tour followed, during which Johnson was introduced to the band's devotees; many found his uncanny similarity to Scott – both vocally and visually – quite chilling. The group's 1981 album, *For Those About To Rock (We Salute You)*, however, sounded weak and hurried, while *Flick Of The Switch* (1983) was also lacking in power.

In 1983, AC/DC lost their last real link with Australia when drummer Phil Rudd departed, to be replaced by young Englishman Simon Wright from the Manchester group Tytan (bassist Mark Evans had been replaced by Cliff Williams, from the English band Home, in 1977). Not that these personnel changes affected the band's sound; AC/DC had always been dominated by Angus Young's fiery guitar and, although their latter albums had been weak, the group remained an awesome force on stage. Another world tour followed in 1984, and 1985 saw the release of the LP *Fly On The Wall* and an appearance at the Rock In Rio festival. In essence, their music had not changed, and neither had the relationship with their denim-clad fans – AC/DC still took great pains to maintain a very real level of contact with their public.

Three more top-selling albums— *Fly On The Wall* (1985), *Who Made Who* (1986) and *Blow Up Your Video* (1988) ensured that fan following remained as strong as ever.

AC/DC
Recommended Listening
Highway To Hell (Atlantic K50628) (Includes: Highway To Hell, Walk All Over You, Touch Too Much, If You Want Blood (You've Got It), Shot Down In Flames); *Back In Black* (Atlantic K50735) (Includes: Hell's Bells, Have A Drink On Me, You Shook Me All Night Long).

Far left: Angus Young commits hara-kiri on the cover of If You Want Blood You've Got It (1978). Left: Vocalist Brian Johnson who replaced Scott. Below: Angus raises his axe to the heavens during a typically demented AC/DC show.

THE IRON AGE

Hammerblows from Iron Maiden's forge

'THE WAY THAT Iron Maiden is, we are going to be like those bands that can still supply the goods after a long time. We are not the sort of band that is going to be big-headed as we've come from working-class backgrounds and we don't care if we play Madison Square Garden or the Marquee.' Bass-guitarist Steve Harris' 1981 predictions for Iron Maiden, the band he founded in June 1976, emphasised the qualities of determination and loyalty to their fans that helped take the band to the head of the 'new wave' of British heavy metal.

Breaking through
An iron maiden was a medieval instrument of torture, a metal, coffin-like device with strategically placed spikes in its lid, which was then closed on its victim; it was Harris' dream that this band's music should have similarly penetrative properties. However, as the band hustled for pub gigs in East London, Harris (born 12 March 1957 in Leytonstone, London) found it hard to keep a stable line-up for long. His most regular cohort at this time was former Urchin guitarist Dave Murray (born 23 December 1958 in Clapton, London).

During the winter of 1978, Steve and Dave, joined by vocalist Paul Di'anno (born 17 May 1959 in Chingford, Essex) and drummer Doug Sampson, went into Cambridge's Spaceward Studios to

record a four-track demo – 'Iron Maiden', 'Prowler', 'Invasion' and 'Strange World'. They sent a copy to Neal Kay, DJ at the Bandwagon Heavy Metal Soundhouse in Kingsbury, North-west London. Kay was highly impressed with what he heard and invited the band to play at the Soundhouse, where they soon became firm favourites. The tape was subsequently released, minus 'Strange World', as an EP on the independent Rock Hard Records label in the winter of 1979.

With London gigs supporting Motorhead at the Music Machine and a first headlining date at the Marquee on 4 November 1979, Iron Maiden's reputation grew apace. While *Sounds* proudly proclaimed the birth of a 'new wave' of British heavy-metal groups, naming Iron Maiden, Def Leppard and Saxon as its leaders, Iron Maiden were snapped up by EMI and booked into Kingsway Studios to record their debut album.

By this time, Sampson had been forced to leave the group due to health problems. His place was taken by ex-Samson drummer Clive Burr (born 8 March 1957 in East Ham, London), while former Remus Down Boulevard guitarist Dennis Stratton (born 9 November 1954 in Canning Town, London) joined.

Above: Dave Murray (left), Steve Harris (centre) and Adrian Smith hammer out some iron-hard riffs. Far left: Iron Maiden's original vocalist Paul Di'anno in action. Di'anno left the group in mid-1981, and was replaced by former Samson singer Bruce Dickinson (left).

Iron Maiden (1980) was produced by Will Malone and included new versions of 'Prowler' and 'Iron Maiden' as well as 'Strange World'. The production left much to be desired, however, having a very trebly sound, but on the plus side, the LP cover sported the distinctive artwork of Derek Riggs. This was to become an instantly recognisable part of Iron Maiden's image, and featured the band's manic 'mascot', Eddie the Head.

Thank you

A month before the LP's release, the band supported Judas Priest on tour, one of the groups that Harris had idolised in the early Seventies. Iron Maiden's explosive performances helped to win them plenty of friends and ensure healthy sales for their album, which made Number 4 in the UK.

Iron Maiden hardly paused for breath before going back on the road on their Sanctuary Tour, their first as headliners, with Praying Mantis as support. The tour climaxed with a sell-out gig at London's Rainbow Theatre and three dates at the Marquee as a 'thank you' to the fans who had been with them from the beginning. After playing a few further dates in Europe, the band returned to the UK to make a special guest appearance at the Reading Festival.

Running out of steam

With the music world apparently convinced of Iron Maiden's success in their field, Dennis Stratton dramatically tendered his resignation from the band due to 'musical differences'. Although he was speedily replaced by Adrian Smith, one of Dave Murray's former companions in Urchin, Iron Maiden's fortunes went into a decline. Their second LP, *Killers* (1981), entered the charts at Number 10, but gained only mixed reviews. While the production by Martin Birch (whose past credits included Deep Purple and Whitesnake) was superior to that of their debut, the band seemed to be having difficulty writing new songs. All but four of the LP's 10 tracks had been recorded before and the several live cuts lacked the sparkle of Iron Maiden's earlier showings. Di'anno's voice

Below: The Piece Of Mind *album added an inflatable brain to the stage set. Bottom: Vocalist Bruce Dickinson is joined on stage by Iron Maiden's grotesque playmate Eddie the Head.*

had sounded weak and strained, and it was no surprise to learn, in mid 1981, that he had parted company with the band.

His replacement was former Samson vocalist Bruce Bruce, who reverted to his real name of Bruce Dickinson when he joined Iron Maiden. A traditional, heavy-metal singer in the style of Robert Plant and Ian Gillan, his approach contrasted markedly with that of Di'anno, whose singing had been punkier. Dickinson made his British debut with the group at a half-empty Rainbow Theatre in London at the end of 1981.

Iron Maiden were to regain their lost popularity, however, following the release of the poppy chant 'Run To The Hills', which made Number 7 in the UK charts. The band's 1982 tour became a sell-out; when they headlined at the Hammersmith Odeon, London, on 20 March, touts were asking upwards of £15 a ticket.

The beginning of April saw the release of their third studio LP *The Number Of The Beast* (1982), produced once more by Martin Birch. A Number 1 hit in the UK charts, the LP showed that the group was still capable of writing fine songs, 'Hallowed Be Thy Name' and '22, Acacia Avenue' being particularly outstanding.

Sweet dreams

The Number Of The Beast was the first LP by the band to make a significant impact on the huge American market, and Iron Maiden spent much of 1982 in the US, returning briefly to England to play the Reading Festival. With a growing Stateside following, Iron Maiden were now in the superstar league and seemed in danger of losing contact with their 'working-class' roots. In keeping with their new luxury, tax-exile lifestyle, they chose to record their fourth album, *Piece Of Mind* (1983), in the Bahamas, with Martin Birch again producing. By now, Clive Burr had left the group and been replaced by ex-Pat Travers and Trust drummer Nicko McBrain. The album entered the UK charts at Number 3 and made the US Top 20 LP charts.

1984's *Powerslave* impressively included Egyptian influences with the more usual sword and sorcery themes, while the live set *Live After Death* (1985) saw Maiden in their element. The following year's contribution *Somewhere in Time* was equally impressive.

But they recognised that too much touring was in danger of dulling their edge, and an interval elapsed before a triumphant return in 1988 with *Seventh Son Of A Seventh Son*. Ten years on, Maiden still ruled the heavy metal roost.

**Iron Maiden
Recommended Listening**

Number Of The Beast (EMI EMC 3400) (Includes: Invaders, The Number Of The Beast, Hallowed Be They Name, Run To The Hills, The Prisoner, Children Of The Damned); *Piece Of Mind* (EMI EMA 800) (Includes: Die With Your Boots On, The Trooper, Flight Of Icarus, Quest For Fire, Sun And Steel, Revelations).

Neil Peart (left), Alex Lifeson (centre) and Geddy Lee before the Rush logo which some critics believed to be 'crypto-fascist'.

Master plans for tomorrow's world

RUSH HAVE BEEN described as a poor imitation of groups as diverse as Black Sabbath, King Crimson, Grand Funk Railroad and Yes. They have been branded as crypto-fascists and, in one memorable turn of phrase, Paul Du Noyer of *New Musical Express* described their lyrics and philosophy as 'an ill-argued dog's dinner of Plato, Milton Friedman and Patience Strong'. At the same time, Rush have been lauded as 'awe-inspiring', 'the very best in their genre', 'expert, awesome, energetic and aware', 'members of an élite circle at the pinnacle of international rock' and 'one of the foremost musical forces and performing ensembles in the world'.

High-school rock
Founder members Geddy Lee (vocals, bass guitar, keyboards) and Alex Lifeson (lead guitar) met at school in Sarnia, a small township in the Canadian province of Ontario a couple of hundred miles from Toronto. Lee was born in Willowdale in the same province, while Lifeson came from Fernie in British Columbia. Together with drummer John Rutsey they formed a band at high school, singing songs by bands such as Grand Funk Railroad, the Jimi Hendrix Experience, Iron Butterfly and Cream.

They played at school dances and private parties, graduating at the start of the Seventies to the bar and club circuit, which had been given a boost by new government legislation that lowered the legal drinking age from 21 to 18.

The band had earlier met up with a young promoter called Ray Danniels who had fixed them up with a gig in an Ontario school. When Danniels and his partner Vic Wilson got the chance to put the New York Dolls on at the Maple Leaf Gardens in Toronto in 1973 they remembered Rush and added them as support act.

Despite being daunted by the large audience, Rush went down well and decided to capitalise on this success by recording an album. Danniels and Wilson raised the money for the studio time and employed a local producer for the sessions, but the results were disastrous and Rush and their managers decided to bring in Terry Brown, who could boast extensive production experience with groups like April Wine, Thundermug and Procol Harum. Brown and Rush went into the Toronto Sound Studios and spent 9000 dollars on studio time, emerging with an infinitely better product.

Despite all their efforts, no record company would sign the group, so Rush and their managers decided to release their LP, *Rush* (1974), on their own label, which they called Moon Records. The

album was available only in and around Toronto, but the first pressings sold out quickly due to the band's reputation as a hard-rocking live act.

Then came one of those lucky strokes of fate that most successful bands can boast of in their history. A friend of the group sent a copy of *Rush* to Donna Halper, the musical director of radio station WMMS, Cleveland, Ohio. She was so impressed by both the record and the response from her listeners that she informed both Mercury Records and New York talent agency ATI of Rush's remarkable potential. Both organisations signed Rush up in the summer of 1974 – Mercury, no doubt, heartened by the success of another Canadian band they already had on their roster, Bachman Turner Overdrive. Rush earned a two-album deal from Mercury worth 200,000 dollars. By the end of the year *Rush* had sold 75,000 copies – not a bad achievement for a debut album from a Canadian band.

Return to fantasy
Within a month of the album's release, however, Rush were faced with the urgent problem of finding a replacement for John Rutsey in order to fulfil the dates of an extensive tour of the US arranged by ATI. He had been forced to quit the group because of ill-health brought on by the gruelling touring schedules that Rush had set themselves since turning professional. After auditioning dozens of hopefuls, Lee and Lifeson eventually decided to enlist Neil Peart, whom they remembered from the Toronto club circuit.

Peart was born and raised near Toronto. An extensive reader, he was particularly attracted to fantasy and science fiction, most notably by such authors as C. S. Lewis, J. R. R. Tolkien and the Russian-born, Canadian-naturalised Ayn Rand, who was to prove a prodigious influence on both Peart and Rush.

As a child Peart showed an interest in music, which his parents attempted to satisfy by sending him to piano lessons. Unfortunately the piano was not the instrument he had in mind, so they eventually ended up buying him a drum kit and 18 months' worth of lessons. Having played in high-school and club bands, Peart tried his luck in London, a city he considered as something of a musical home given his interest in drummers like Keith Moon, Carl Palmer, and Bill Bruford. Things did not work out for him there, however, and he was reduced to selling souvenirs on sleazy Carnaby Street. He eventually packed his bags and headed for home, where he finally joined Rush.

Rush's first tour of the US ran from the middle of August to just before December 1974, playing bills headed by such bands as Manfred Mann's Earth Band, Uriah Heep, Rory Gallagher and Blue Cheer. The reviews of Rush's concerts were mixed, but the band were undismayed. Their debut LP had proved to be Mercury's biggest-selling first album by a Canadian group;

this fact encouraged them to return to the studios in January 1975 to work on a follow-up.

At this point Peart revealed that the band had got much more than a talented percussionist when they signed him up. He proved to be a gifted ideas man and a hard-working lyricist. The band's second album, *Fly By Night*, immediately showed Peart's influence, featuring tracks with epic or mythological themes, such as 'By-Tor And The Snow Dog', 'Rivendell' (the name of a village in Tolkien's *Lord Of The Rings*) and the notorious 'Anthem', inspired by Ayn Rand's 1938 novel of the same name.

The last-named song became notorious because Ms Rand was considered by some to be something of a fascist in her views. With its emphasis on free will, personal responsibility and dislike of socialism, 'Anthem' and a number of similar songs were to earn Rush the title of 'crypto-fascists' from some left-wing music critics in the late Seventies. Peart has vehemently and repeatedly denied any such leanings: 'I'm not a fascist or an extremist. I'm a capitalist and I believe in self-reliance – that's all.'

Fly By Night was rapidly completed, being released in February 1975. At the same time, Rush won a Juno Award, Canada's equivalent to the Grammy, for being the country's most promising new group. With the album selling well and the Juno award on their mantelpiece, Rush embarked on their second US tour, supporting Kiss and Aerosmith.

They then went back into the studios in Toronto to work on their third album, *Caress Of Steel* (1975). While the album included a nonsense song called 'I Think I'm Going Bald', a melodic gem entitled 'Lakeside Park', and a further instalment in the legend of By-Tor in 'Necromancer', its most important feature was that the whole of one side was devoted to 'The Fountain Of Lamneth'. This epic track combined all of Peart's influences and ideas in a single glorious outpouring. With hindsight, 'The Fountain Of Lamneth' now seems overstuffed with themes and allegories, but at the time it underlined the fact that Rush were considerably more than just another heavy-metal band.

By the end of March 1976 *Fly By Night* had gone gold in Canada, while in the same country *Caress Of Steel* had sold 40,000 copies – a fine achievement ·since it had been released only the previous September. Heartened by the success of both albums, Rush decided to be even more ambitious with their next release. It was left to Peart to come up with the subject-matter and, once again, he turned to Ayn Rand and her novel *Anthem*. He concentrated on the lyrics, while Lee and Lifeson worked together on the music. The material took six months to compile and a month to record – the result was *2112*.

Released in late 1976, the album concerned the battle of an individual against a world run by the despotic Priests of the Temple of Syrinx, where society was governed by logic and anything illogical – including music – was outlawed.

Rush's portrayal of this totalitarian state infuriated some critics, who were also quick to read special significance into Rush's logo – a naked man fending off a *red* star. Peart and Rush remained unperturbed, however, considering *2112* the culmination of their achievements. Admitting that the album had exhausted them of ideas, the band came up with a live album for their next release. It was called *All The World's A Stage*, recorded at Toronto's Massey Hall and released in the autumn of 1976.

Rush through time

Both *2112* and *All The World's A Stage* established Rush as a major band in the US and also initiated their acceptance in the UK. Their growing transatlantic popularity was cemented in the middle of 1977 when they played their first dates in Britain and Europe. Earlier in the year, they had come to Britain to record *A Farewell To Kings* (1977) in Rockfield Studios in Wales.

Previous Rush albums had been available in the UK only on a limited-edition import policy adopted by Phonogram, the company that handled Mercury's releases there. Rush's British sales figures had eventually proved sufficiently heartening for *A Farewell To Kings* to be officially released in the UK, and the group's previous albums subsequently saw belated release. Rush's stature increased with the release of each of their subsequent LPs – *Hemispheres* (1978), *Permanent Waves*

Opposite: Alex Lifeson (left) and Geddy Lee rock out at the double. Below: All the world's a stage – and Rush take it by storm.

(1980), *Moving Pictures* (1981), their second live album *Exit . . . Stage Left* (1981) and *Signals* (1982).

There were no dramatic line-up changes in the band after Peart joined, nor any dramatic announcements about a change of approach or direction either on stage or on record. Instead, Rush pursued a policy of gradual development that culminated with the release of *Signals*, a marvellous collection of hugely disparate elements – everything from hints of Peart's old sword-and-sorcery confections to reggae.

Their popularity in the UK was such that in 1982 Rush played to capacity audiences for two nights at the enormous National Exhibition Centre in Birmingham and three nights at London's Wembley Arena. Their successful output has continued with the release of the 1984 LP *Grace Under Pressure* and *Power Windows* in late 1985, with *Hold Your Fire* as a 1987 contribution.

Commenting on the status that Rush have achieved, Geddy Lee has said: 'It's been a long time since we could have been considered a heavy-metal band, if ever. And it's just as long since we could have been called a "pomp-rock" band or a "progressive band" or whatever. We are our own men with our own tastes. We have dozens of interests and influences and we intend to show them for a long time to come.'   BRIAN HARRIGAN

Rush
Recommended Listening

Rush Through Time (Mercury 6337 171) (Includes: Fly By Night, Anthem, Closer To The Heart, Bastille Day, Overture/Temples Of Syrinx, Something For Nothing); *Exit . . . Stage Left* (Mercury 6619 053) (Includes: The Spirit Of Radio, YYZ, The Trees, Tom Sawyer, A Passage To Bangkok, La Ville Strangiato).

Burning down the house with Def Leppard

CERTAIN PARALLELS could be drawn between the punk revolution of the late Seventies and the 'new wave' of British heavy-metal bands that followed swiftly on its heels. Although the fact that punk derived much of its impact from the social and political concerns of its lyrics contrasted with the purely escapist notions inherent in the majority of heavy-metal anthems, there was nevertheless a number of common sources to the two musical styles.

Both derived inspiration from the teen-age music and lyrics of the same early-Seventies acts. For the new heavy-metal bands, the common sources of Slade, Bowie, T.Rex and Alice Cooper often proved as influential as Led Zeppelin and Deep Purple. It is arguable that, in the public eye, punk created the greater moral outcry because their clothes represented a stand against convention, whereas the attire of the hard-rock fan was based purely on the comfort of a ready-to-wear pair of jeans and a T-shirt.

Steel appeal

Born and raised in Sheffield, Britain's foremost steel-producing city, the members of Def Leppard faced the dilemma of playing escapist music in a city that was fast getting a name for breeding discontented bands challenging the social status quo. Their first line-up comprised vocalist Joe Elliott, guitarist Pete Willis and bassist Rick Savage. They cut their teeth on the heavy-metal hits of the day – Thin Lizzy's 'Jailbreak' and Bob Seger's 'Rosalie' among them – before the addition of second guitarist Steve Clark gave them the incentive to expand their repertoire to include self-penned numbers.

With the line-up completed by 15-year-old schoolboy drummer Rick Allen, they set about recording their self-financed *Getcha Rocks Off* EP, released in 1979 on their own Bludgeon Riffola label. In terms of recording quality, *Getcha Rocks Off* compared favourably with the punk indies and brought the band much favourable publicity.

It was around this time that Geoff Barton, long-time standard bearer for heavy rock in the pages of *Sounds*, drew attention to the fanatical yet insular heavy-metal underground. In clubs the length and breadth of the UK, denim and leather-clad metal fans were gathering each week to listen to the music of mega-bands like Judas Priest, UFO and the Scorpions on disc. Now, bands like Leppard, Iron Maiden, Angelwitch, More and Samson provided a chance to see well-played heavy metal in an accessible live setting. The response to this initiative was, perhaps predictably, enthusiastic.

Although Leppard made few friends in their first *Sounds* interview with their outspokenness and uncompromising attitude, their desire to play aggressive yet

melodic rock was obvious, and provided the first indication of their leaning towards the American market. Vocalist and spokesman Joe Elliott never made a secret of his disappointment that America took Leppard to its heart while British fans seemed to regard the band as 'traitors' pursuing a quick buck.

The wave breaks

Being the first of the 'new wave' of heavy bands to sign a major deal (with Phonogram), all eyes were on the band – and although not a classic debut album, *On Through The Night* (1980) reflected the band's live show and objectives. The

album's one major failing was Judas Priest producer Tom Allom's relegation of the dynamics of Pete Willis' and Steve Clark's normally dazzling guitar interplay so far back in the mix as to sound almost nonexistent. The album peaked at Number 15 in the UK charts, but could have achieved a higher placing had the production been more sympathetic.

Being the first new young heavy-rock band to put out an album, Leppard carried the can for the entire movement and reviews were quick to point out the record's shortcomings. To avoid further critical flak, they set off for the United States, where they felt they would receive a fairer

Above: Leppard roar into action, from left Steve Clark, Rick Savage, Phil Collen, Rick Allen and Joe Elliott. Despite the patriotic nature of the singer's garb, it was in the US rather than in their native Britain that the band found most success.

hearing. After a seemingly endless tour, they re-entered the studio to record their second album, *High'n'Dry* (1981), with producer Robert John 'Mutt' Lange of AC/DC fame. The results were immediately obvious. Not only were the guitars sounding individual yet sympathetic, but Rick Savage's hard-hitting and solid bass playing now sounded as if it had been recorded on the same planet as the drums.

If the bass and guitars sounded leaps and bounds better than *On Through The Night*, then the drums and vocals sounded as if there had been a line-up change. Gone was the nondescript thud of Rick Allen's seemingly arthritic snare and bass drum spasms, to be replaced with a driving crack that propelled the songs along at what seemed a live pace, while the guts and bravado of the vocals gave the lyrics a much-needed edge.

Leppard then set out on another British tour. Although the band's critics were still in evidence, Leppard had come back from the States as a far more professional band with style, stage presence and aggression. As a result of the *High'n'Dry* tour, they were slowly but surely beating a critical backlash that had inspired a barrage of beer cans at their 1980 Reading Festival appearance, but the new album still only made Number 26 in the LP charts. The subsequent Stateside tour, however, transformed Leppard almost overnight from an up-and-coming British band into a headlining act.

Burning sounds

It was time for another album to consolidate these gains and, deciding once again to use Mutt Lange, they had to wait nearly a year for him to fulfil his prior commitments. By the time the band got into the studio, they had assembled a number of promising songs that threatened to make the forthcoming album the best to date. Although credited as co-writer of almost half the songs and laying down some inspired backing tracks on the album, guitarist and founder member Pete Willis decided that he had had enough and returned to Sheffield.

Phil Collen, ex-Girl guitarist and an old friend, was at the same time trying to put a band together. Phil was given a backing tape to one of the songs and told that if he came back the next day with an adequate solo then he had the job. The completed album, on release, attested to the success of Collen's efforts, and he was confirmed as a member shortly afterwards.

In terms of recorded material, *Pyromania* (1983) was the logical extension of *High'n'Dry*, both production and songs complementing each other perfectly to make it without doubt the most listenable of their albums. 'Rock Of Ages' was a US Top Twenty single, while the LP's 'tailored for radio' sound undoubtedly assisted it in keeping it in the Top Five of the US album chart for much of 1983. In the UK, however, it went straight into the chart at Number 18 but progressed no further.

The US video channel MTV had been responsible for helping to bridge the eighteen-month gap between albums by continually playing three of Leppard's promotional videos. The band's popularity received a further boost as they toured, with the result that, as *Pyromania* was released early in 1983, sales of *High'n'Dry* had nearly doubled since the touring started. The success of *Pyromania* was eventually exceeded by 1987's *Hysteria*, delayed by a road accident which saw drummer Rick Allen playing with an arm amputated. But Def Leppard were not going to quit just yet!   GEOFF BANKS

Def Leppard
Recommended Listening

High'n'Dry (Vertigo 6359 045) (Includes: Another Hit And Run, High'n'Dry (Saturday Night), Lady Strange, You Got Me Runnin', Let It Go, No No No); *Pyromania* (Vertigo VERS 2) (Includes: Photograph, Rock Of Ages, Action! Not Words, Comin' Under Fire, Rock! Rock! (Till You Drop), Stagefright).

WHITE L

Life in the fast lane with Motorhead

THE PRIMAL BEAUTY of Motorhead is like that of a shipwreck or plane crash: 'Iron Fist', 'Overkill', 'Limb From Limb' – their song titles say it all. The simple rhythms of destruction reflect a nostalgia for a mythical world where boys are bred to kill and girls are bred to breed.

Motorhead's driving force, a shambling, gap-toothed greaser called Lemmy, was born plain Ian Kilminster in Blackpool in 1945. The son of a vicar, he reputedly acquired his nickname through his habit of asking people to 'lemme a fiver'. His first professional band was the Rockin' Vickers – named after a machine gun – and in 1968 he joined the fashionably Indian-style Sam Gopal band. In those days, he played rhythm and lead guitar.

After a spell as a roadie for, among others, Jimi Hendrix, Lemmy joined the psychedelic bikers' band Hawkwind as a bass player in 1972. He was soon writing songs for the band, and sang on their 1972 UK Number 3 hit 'Silver Machine'. But in 1975 Canadian customs officials found some amphetamine sulphate – which they thought was cocaine – about his person and he was unceremoniously sacked from the group, who feared his drugs record would endanger their tour.

Motorhead tune up

Back in England, Lemmy's old friend, journalist/musician Mick Farren, introduced him to drummer Lucas Fox and former Pink Fairies guitarist Larry Wallis: with these two, Lemmy decided to form a band called Bastard. On the advice of manager Doug Smith, however, he agreed to change the name to Motorhead, US slang for a speed (amphetamine) freak, and the title of a song Lemmy had written during his last days with Hawkwind. He outlined the new group's prospectus: 'They'll be the dirtiest rock'n'roll band in the world. If we moved in next door to you your lawn would die.'

Motorhead made their debut at London's Roundhouse on 20 July 1975, supporting Greenslade. The set included 'Motorhead' and 'Lost Johnny', later to become live favourites. With the trio's combined heritage, the gig attracted quite a lot of interest. Unfortunately, their next prestige date, with Blue Oyster Cult at the Hammersmith Odeon, suffered from a bad sound system and lack of rehearsal. The papers, not yet bitten by the punk bug, gave Motorhead a critical dive-bombing from which few groups would have recovered.

Lemmy was still under contract to United Artists, and it was for that label that Motorhead recorded an album in the winter of 1975. But Lemmy was still not satisfied with the personnel, and he persuaded his friend Phil 'Philthy Animal' Taylor, a reggae and Motown fan who had never drummed professionally before, to overdub drums onto the album. Lucas Fox was erased from the band as he was erased from the tape, and Phil was in. But UA were non-committal about the album. Under the typical pretext of 'seeing about the photographs' they effectively shelved the record altogether, although they would not let the band sign for any other label.

At this point 'Fast' Eddie Clarke came on the scene. He had met Phil while renovating an old barge, and when the idea of a second guitarist was mooted by the band, Eddie's name was brought up. Clarke had previously played for Curtis Knight – who was best-known for once having played with Jimi Hendrix – and in a group called Blue Goose, but had never had the chance to play with a recording band: he was so keen to impress that he paid for the rehearsal time, and was content to play second guitar to Larry Wallis when the latter finally deigned to appear. After half-an-hour or so, Wallis just turned off his amp and walked out of the band, leaving the new Motorhead in place at last.

As the UA album gathered dust, and the band's relations with the company stagnated, Jake Riviera suggested to Lemmy that they do an informal, one-off single for his new Stiff label. Accordingly, the band recorded 'White Line Fever', one of their first trio compositions, and 'Leavin' Here', a Motown oldie. At the last minute, however, UA invoked their still-existing contract to block the release. It surfaced later in compilation and boxed-set forms, but to Motorhead, still without a record release, the frustration was becoming unbearable. They decided to split up, and asked Ted Carroll, Svengali of the other main UK independent label, Chiswick, to record their last gig. To their amazement, Carroll told them after the gig that he had not recorded it, and asked them to record a single.

At this point, several factors remained in Motorhead's favour. The 'new wave' of British heavy metal had not yet broken, and hard rock was still in the hands of acts like Frankie Miller and Bad Company. But Motorhead's combination of speed and volume endeared them to rock and punk fans alike. Second, United Artists had finally dropped them. Third, they worked so fast in the studio that in the two days Chiswick gave them to do a single, they recorded 13 backing tracks. On hearing them, Ted Carroll authorised them to complete an album, which duly surfaced as *Motorhead* in August 1977.

The band were given another push by

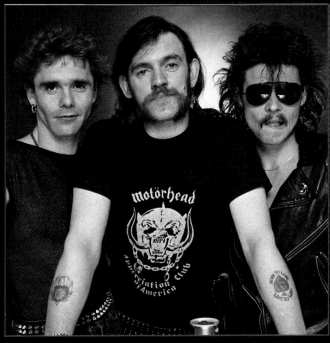

Above: Motorhead in 1983, from left Brian Robertson, Lemmy Kilminster and 'Philthy Animal' Taylor. Opposite: Kilminster prepares for lift-off.

the arrival on the scene of legendary Sixties supremo Tony Secunda, who proved very useful for a while on the promotional front. The name 'Motorhead' was emblazoned on prominent London walls, and a tour was set up, which had to be cancelled after only four dates when Taylor had his wrist broken in a fight. A film was to be made of Motorhead's life, both on and off the road, but Secunda wrecked the movie equiment during a row with the band.

Monster success

He was becoming increasingly unreliable, and after he declared himself bankrupt and returned to the US, the trio returned to their old manager, Doug Smith. Smith procured them a deal with Bronze Records, the first release being an armour-plated version of the old standard 'Louie Louie', which brought them to the national eye on BBC-TV's 'Top Of The Pops', and made Number 68 in the UK.

With the release of their next album *Overkill* (produced by Stones and Traffic veteran Jimmy Miller) in March 1979, Motorhead built up a routine of recording and touring that continued uninterrupted for three years. *Overkill* reached Number 24 in the UK album charts and its successor – *Bomber*, released in 1979 – reached Number 12. On the promotional tour for the latter album, a giant tubular steel representation of a World War II Heinkel bomber, as depicted on the album cover, made its debut. The sight of this monster winging low over the band, to the

accompaniment of taped engine noises, thrilled the fans.

Meanwhile, with the onset of success, UA finally and predictably released their old Motorhead tapes as *On Parole* (1980). The band were less than excited by this flashback to their long-dead first incarnation, but at least it proved that, in the public eye, Motorhead had made it. The highlights of 1980 were the Heavy Metal Brain Damage Party in Stafford, where bill-toppers Motorhead were presented with a silver disc by a look-alike of the Queen, and the tour that followed the Vic Maile-produced *Ace Of Spades* album.

This tour produced the gigs that were recorded for the now-legendary *No Sleep Till Hammersmith* album. With Lemmy's rasping voice backed by Phil's drums, and the fluid screech of Eddie at his fastest, the band finally made it. Within three days of its June 1981 release, the LP reached Number 1 in the UK album chart.

In late 1980, however, Phil and 10 of the roadies were taken in for questioning on suspicion of possessing drugs. Taylor had a further stroke of bad luck when a drunken romp landed him with three cracked neck vertebrae. He was thus unable to play on the *St Valentine's Day Massacre* EP, on which Motorhead and Girlschool joined forces for an update of the old Johnny Kidd and the Pirates tune, 'Please Don't Touch', which made Number 5 in the UK charts in early 1981.

Reflecting their new international status, Motorhead supported megaheavies Blizzard of Oz on a 40-date midsummer tour of the US, returning to Britain to top the Heavy Metal Holocaust bill at Port Vale Football Club. Midway through recording their *Iron Fist* (1982) album, however, they parted company with their long-serving producer Vic Maile, the album suffering as a result.

Then, during their gruelling US tour to promote the album, Clarke suddenly left the band to form Fastway. Thin Lizzy axeman Brian Robertson took his place until the end of 1983, when the album *Another Perfect Day* was released. Taylor then quit 'to take a long overdue rest' and a new band was formed with Saxon drummer Pete Gill and two lead guitarists – Phil Campbell (formerly of Persian Risk) and Wurzel, an ex-army corporal. Four tracks by the new Motorhead appeared on a compilation album *No Remorse*.

Phil Taylor's return was celebrated by *Orgasmatron* (1986) and *Rock'n'Roll*, both on the new GWR label. And 1988's *No Sleep At All*, yet another live set, proved beyond doubt that Motorhead were still in business.   LUTHER PAISLEY

Above: Motorhead with Girlschool. Below: Guitarist 'Fast' Eddie Clark, who left the band in 1982. Left: Lemmy booms.

Motorhead
Recommended Listening

Overkill (Bronze BRON 515) (Includes: I'll Be Your Sister, Capricorn, No Class, Tear Ya Down, Overkill, Damage Case); *Bomber* (Bronze BRON 523) (Includes: Dead Men Tell No Tales, Poison, Stone Dead Forever, Bomber, Talking Head, All The Aces).

Second Time Around

Sixties beat bounced back in the wake of the new wave

To BORROW a well-known catchphrase from the early days of Stiff Records, power pop was very much a case of 'yesterday's sound today'. It fused together some of the best elements of mid-Sixties pop music – the Beatles, Byrds, Kinks, Who, Creation, Easybeats and the like – with contemporary perspectives and production techniques. Initially coined in the mid Seventies by US critic Greg Shaw to describe bands like Big Star, the name was soon to become an umbrella term for such acts as Nick Lowe, the Rich Kids, the Boomtown Rats, the Jam, the Pretenders and other acts with obvious Sixties influences.

Pure pop for now people

By the early Seventies, pop had become something of a dirty word, a synonym for middle-of-the-road recordings that lacked any real substance, with very few musicians showing any interest in a form that had been, in its heyday, the heart of the Top Thirty. Aside from glitter rockers like Sweet, who saw the virtue of the three-minute pop song and tried to put

some fun and excitement back into the proceedings, there were virtually no groups interested in continuing the pop traditions of the mid Sixties. It was not until the onslaught of punk that pop's fortunes began to look up again.

Singles were suddenly back in fashion and the three-minute pop song back in vogue, albeit in a somewhat less melodic form than in the Sixties. The Sex Pistols and contemporaries reached the charts and found a young audience who were searching for new values. While the punks' angry brand of music found commercial success, a few old hands like Nick Lowe borrowed the brash excitement of punk and tailored it to a pop sensibility to produce something akin to 'power pop'. Lowe's 1977 EP *Bowi* described itself as 'Pure pop for now people', indicating that pop music was about to undergo a fresh phase of credibility.

Many of the early punk records were similarly inclined, marrying aggression and passion together with plenty of pop hooks to achieve a commercial sound. The Jam's first hit, 'In The City', had strong overtones of the

Above: Former Sex Pistol Glen Matlock (left) formed the Rich Kids with drummer Rusty Egan, future Ultravox frontman Midge Ure (centre) and Steve New (right). They failed to find public acceptance, however, and split after the release of a single album.

early Who, the Boomtown Rats' first two singles – 'Looking After Number One' and 'Mary Of The Fourth Form' – owed much to the R&B of the early Rolling Stones, while the Pretenders first hit, 'Stop Your Sobbing', was a cover version of an old Kinks' song. But while these three bands managed to develop distinctive styles of their own and achieve high levels of commercial success, there was a whole host of other groups operating in the late Seventies whose strict allegiance to the sounds of the Sixties proved to be an obstacle to musical evolution.

Suits and boots

It was into the volatile environment of 1977 that the Pleasers were born, a band who were to become the face of the power-pop fad. Decked out in dark suits, red Cuban-heel boots, white tab-collar shirts and knitted ties, Steve McNenery (guitar), Bo Benham (bass), Dave Rotchelle (drums) and Chris Alexandra (guitar – later replaced by Nick Powell) were touted as the new Beatles.

They looked and sounded custom-made for the role, as if they had just walked straight out of 1964, with a wholesome, clean-cut image and bright commercial sound that was completely at odds with the over-the-top anti-fashions of punk. Calling their sound 'Thamesbeat', the combo played an updated form of Merseybeat very reminiscent of the Searchers and the Beatles, adding punk vitality to the beat style of old and thus making it more acceptable to the youth of the mid Seventies.

By late 1977, the novelty of punk rock was fading rapidly, and music magazines were searching for a new phenomenon. They were not slow to hype the merits of power pop. Pictures of the Pleasers and other like-minded contemporaries were plastered across the pages of the rock press, and numerous other power-pop outfits were to surface nationwide during the early months of 1978. There were the Smirks from Manchester, whose quirky version of British beat was rewarded with a contract from the American independent label Beserkley; Southend's Tonight dressed the part in suits, white shirts and slender ties and notched up a UK Number 14 hit with 'Drummer Man'; while the Motors, formed by ex-members of pub-rock group Ducks Deluxe Nick Garvey and Andy McMasters, blended punk energy with jangling guitars reminiscent of the Byrds and the Searchers for their single 'Dancing The Night Away'.

The Yachts' debut 45, 'Suffice To Say', was dominated by clean vocal harmonies, Farfisa organ and a very catchy melody, while the Rich Kids, formed by ex-Sex Pistol Glen Matlock and ex-Slik member Midge Ure, drew on a variety of backgrounds from the classy UK Sixties pop of the Small Faces and the Kinks through the glam-rock of the New York Dolls to the teenybop of the Bay City Rollers. And then there were the Stukas, the Jags, Advertising, the Boys, the Boyfriends, the Speedometers, the Sneaks and more . . .

By the spring of 1978, with Nick Lowe's 'I Love The Sound Of Breaking Glass' nearing the top of the UK singles charts, and a whole crowd of new acts bearing the torch for a new, credible brand of pop, it looked as if rock was

entering a new era. But, in fact, the power-pop craze burned out as swiftly as it had arrived. As David Brown wrote in *Sounds*: 'Suddenly no one wants to be called power pop. No sooner had the phrase been established than it became uncool.' The Pleasers failed to capitalise on the initial surge of interest in them and petered out after a couple of flop singles, possibly because both their image and their music lacked any real spark of imagination. The Rich Kids also proved to be something of a spectacular failure; despite their undeniable talent and a handful of strong singles – notably the excellent 'Ghosts Of Princes In Towers', which successfully united a Sixties-style melody with feisty rock and a lavish production courtesy of ex-Bowie sidekick Mick Ronson – they never found public acclaim.

Lost innocence

This lack of commercial success did not deter others from trying the power-pop formula, however, and the latter months of 1978 saw the emergence of the Records, arguably the best British purveyors of the genre. In Will Birch, ex-drummer of the Kursaal Flyers, and guitarist John Wicks, the Records had a highly gifted songwriting team; the group's debut single, 'Starry Eyes', was a vitriolic put-down of the

music industry that mixed a pounding arrangement, full of punk's zest, with the guitar sound that the Byrds had created on 'Eight Miles High'.

The ensuing album, *Shades In Bed* (1979), confirmed the group's promise, with songs like 'Girls That Don't Exist' and 'Up All Night' showing that power pop could be more than just love songs set to a Sixties beat. Despite some popularity in the US, where their record company failed to promote them adequately, the Records failed to take off in their home country – perhaps because, like other bands of that ilk, they could never quite capture the essential naivety and innocence that had been at the heart of the best Sixties pop music.

Power pop didn't completely disappear, however; during the early Eighties it resurfaced in other guises, notably in 'new psychedelic' bands like Mood Six and High Tide and in yet another band of Beatle soundalikes, Scarlet Party, whose lead singer Graham Dye was constantly compared with the young John Lennon. But again, despite their charm, the new power-pop acts met little public acclaim: for, in relying so heavily on the sound and style of the past, they were missing one vital ingredient for sustained commercial success – originality.   NIGEL CROSS

Power-pop roll-call: the Motors (opposite top), Beatle-clones the Pleasers (opposite below) and Elvis Costello soundalikes the Jags (opposite bottom). Below: The Smirks sign on as the boom fades.

THAT'S entertainment

From Mod to Motown with Paul Weller and the Jam

IT WAS DURING the climax of their success in 1982, with a Number 1 album and single behind them, that Paul Weller, the Jam's singer, songwriter and guitarist, seems to have realised that the group was finished. The band's achievements had been impressive; for five years, they had been one of the most vital and exciting British rock bands of the period. They had established a unique rapport with their large audience based on their down-to-earth image and obvious sincerity, while their songs combined sharp social observation and anger and frustration at society's injustices with powerful, Sixties-influenced pop.

But Weller was not content to dwell on past successes. His interest in soul music was a direction he suspected he would be unable to follow within the group. More importantly, for someone who believed in communicating ideas and being judged on his merits, the adulation surrounding the Jam was becoming stifling. 'I wanted all we have achieved to stand for something,' Weller explained to the fans in a statement printed in the music press. 'The longer a group continues the more frightening the thought of ever ending it becomes – that is why so many of them carry on until they become meaningless. I've never wanted the Jam to get to this stage.'

Jamming in the city
The Jam developed from a schoolboy outfit started by Weller (born 25 May 1958) and his best friend Steve Brookes in their home town of Woking, Surrey. They drafted in Dave Waller, another friend from school, and then an older drummer, Rick Buckler (born 6 December 1955). Waller soon left, being replaced by another schoolfriend,

Bruce Foxton (born 1 September 1955); he originally played guitar, but soon exchanged it for Paul's bass.

Paul's father John had encouraged his son from the beginning and was now acting as their manager; he realised that the band would have to break into the London club circuit if they were ever to get away from playing rock'n'roll covers and soul songs at weddings and Woking pubs. Luckily, he managed to fix up the occasional gig at the Greyhound pub in Fulham, where he knew the manager. While they were paying their dues around the London pub and club scene – meanwhile saying goodbye to Steve Brookes, who was not that keen on becoming a pop star – Paul, at the time a Mod, had his first encounter with punk.

The message that the Clash were hammering home about the gulf between rock stars and their audience seemed particularly pertinent to him – and it was that same group, breakfasting in a nearby café, who witnessed one of the Jam's more audacious stunts when they simply set up and started playing in Soho Market one Saturday morning. That market performance attracted some complimentary press attention and, after a few more months gigging at clubs like the Roxy, the 100 Club and the Nashville, they were signed to the Polydor label early in 1977 for the ludicrously small sum of £6000.

Their first single, 'In The City', was released in April 1977 and reached Number 40 after an appearance on BBC-TV's 'Top Of The Pops'; an album of the same name, which was quickly knocked together and released in May 1977, made it to Number 20. The opening chords of the first track, 'Art School', echoed 'Out In The Street', the first track on the Who's debut album My Generation (1965), indicating a major influence on Weller's songwriting and guitar-playing: he even chose to play

the semi-acoustic Rickenbacker guitars made popular by Pete Townshend in the Sixties. Weller's early work, and some of the later material, was crammed with the jangling harmonies and brash lyrics of the Sixties groups the Woking schoolboy had discovered as an alternative to the contemporary glam-rock scene he hated.

Many of Weller's early songs offered vivid glimpses of teenage street life and, like Pete Townshend before him, the young lyricist appointed himself as a spokesman for his generation. Townshend was later to point out the similarities between them: 'Paul Weller takes on the whole of British society without a blink . . . he's a big-headed, arrrogant little bugger, exactly how I was at his age.'

This fascination with the Sixties also contributed to the failure of the group's first American tour in 1978. Like another of Weller's heroes, Ray Davies of the Kinks, his songs were simply too English to interest an American audience. Not until their final studio album, The Gift (1982), would they begin to do reasonably well in the US charts.

Music for moderns
In Britain, meanwhile, the group were making shaky progress. With some pushing from John Weller, who remained their manager for the group's entire career, they sold out London's Hammersmith Odeon, but their chart success was not quite so spectacular. There were two more singles that year: 'All Around The World', which reached Number 13, and 'The Modern World', which borrowed a riff from the Who's 'Pictures Of Lily' and stuck at Number 36. There was also a second, not particularly inspiring album, This Is The Modern World, that appeared in November 1977 and made Number 22 in the LP charts. Weller was having trouble producing material, and their fourth single was a Bruce Foxton composition, 'News Of The World' which, released in February 1978, only reached Number 23. By the spring of 1978, after a second unsuccessful American tour, the Jam were beginning to look like nine-day wonders.

Part of the trouble seems to have stemmed from Weller's love affair with a girl called Gill, whom he had met during the Jam's first British tour. They moved into a flat together in London's Baker Street, and Weller found himself losing the singlemindedness that had once taken his career from strength to strength. Seeing the writing on the wall, he moved back to his parents' house in Woking – maintaining his relationship with Gill, which was to oulive the Jam – and began to concentrate on his music once more. As a result, the Jam made a slow climb back to popularity with two hit singles, a cover of the Ray Davies song 'David Watts' that made Number 25 and 'Down In The Tube Station At Midnight'. This angry and moving song – about a vicious racial attack – was released in October, and reached Number 15 in the charts.

It was followed by one of the Jam's finest albums, *All Mod Cons* (1978). Invigorated by his break from composing and fuelled by his anger at the British class system, Weller was beginning to find his own voice as a songwriter. Songs like '"A" Bomb In Wardour Street', 'Mr Clean' and 'Down In The Tube Station At Midnight' presented vivid, angry slices of everyday life, while 'English Rose' and 'The Place I Love' offered a dreamy, idyllic contrast. More than almost any songwriter since Ray Davies, Weller had an eye for the details of everyday life: 'They smelt of pubs and Wormwood Scrubs/And too many right-wing meetings,' he sang on 'Tube Station'. It was a gift he was to develop on later songs like 'Saturday's Kids' and 'That's Entertainment'.

Around this time, Weller seems to have decided that if the Jam were to stay successful, it would have to become his group

The Jam in classic Mod pose, from left bassist Bruce Foxton, guitarist Paul Weller and drummer Rick Buckler.

completely. 'From All *Mod Cons* on, I never let go of the leading reins again,' he told the group's biographer, Paolo Hewitt. And, indeed, most of Weller's compositions that were not written in a hurry in the studio were first recorded in demo form with Weller himself playing all the instruments, so that the others would know exactly what sound he wanted. But since Bruce and Rick were allowed to interpret their own parts to some extent, the finished songs were never quite as Weller had envisaged them; and his disappointment with the results was another reason for the Jam's eventual break-up.

The Jam released three singles in 1979: March's 'Strange Town' reached Number 15 and its B-side, 'Butterfly Collector', showed a new, melancholy side to Weller's songwriting; September's 'When You're Young' was a Number 13 hit, and 'Eton Rifles', a wonderfully tragi-comic look at class warfare, shot to Number 3 late in the year.

odd to many people that at this advanced stage in his career he should have been producing songs so reminiscent of other people's work.

Underneath its brash pop-art cover, that year's *Sound Affects* album also displayed a strong hippie influence. Having recently read books by Aldous Huxley and Geoffrey Ash, Weller was trying to express the idea that 'material goals had hidden the spiritual ones and clouded our perceptions'.

The opening track, 'Pretty Green', set a lyric about the power of money to an almost folk-song-like melody, while 'Man In The Corner Shop', 'Set The House Ablaze' and the bitterly sarcastic 'That's Entertainment' – which later charted in the UK as a German import single – continued the Jam tradition of social realism. 'Monday', in contrast, was a hauntingly beautiful, Sixties-style love song. Alongside the previously audible influences of the Kinks, the Who and the Beatles, a touch of Motown could be heard on numbers like 'Boy About Town'.

Their fourth LP, *Setting Sons*, released in October, was intended as a concept album about three boyhood friends growing up and growing apart. Several of the songs – 'Thick As Thieves', 'Little Boy Soldiers', 'Wasteland' and 'Burning Sky' – did stick to this plan, while others, like 'Saturday's Kids', were bleak snapshots of English life. Weller's anger at the British class system was as clear as ever; but on *Setting Sons* it was tinged with a sense of frustration and disillusionment that made this the Jam's harshest and gloomiest LP. The album's strongest – and most frightening – song was 'Private Hell', a grim depiction of a middle-aged woman's emotional disintegration as her children leave home.

But Weller lacked the time to complete the concept, so the album was padded out with fillers like 'Girl On The Phone' and a cover of Martha and the Vandellas' 'Heatwave', much to its detriment. The band

The Jam's smart mohair suits (above) later gave way to a more casual, less deliberately Sixties look (below).

were bitterly disappointed with the result, although the album reached Number 4 in the charts.

Psychedelic sounds

1980 was a different story. The Jam's March single, 'Going Underground', helped by some sharp marketing from Polydor, went straight in at Number 1, while their follow-up single, 'Start', also made the top spot. The song bore more than a passing resemblance to George Harrison's 'Taxman' on the Beatles' *Revolver* album of 1966, and promotional pictures appeared of the group in psychedelic granny glasses. Weller's explanation was that he'd been 'listening to *Revolver* a lot recently', but it seemed

Starting over

Sound Affects was also the end of the road for producer Vic Coppersmith. His careful perfectionism had started to infuriate Weller, who preferred to work much more spontaneously in the studio. Coppersmith had worked on all five Jam albums, the first two in conjunction with Chris Parry who had originally signed the group to Polydor. There was no urgent need for a replacement, however, since the group – bored and fed-up – had decided to take most of 1981 off. Apart from the unmemorable group composition 'Funeral Pyre', a Number 4 hit in the middle of the year, no more was heard from them until their thirteenth single, 'Absolute Beginners', was released in October 1981, and also charted at Number 4.

That record, although no one realised it at the time, was the beginning of the end. Behind the hints on 'Absolute Beginners' of Weller's revived interest in black music – particularly the horns well up in the mix – was his new ambition to develop and progress in a soul direction, something he thought would be impossible within the Jam. Over the previous year, he had also become immersed in projects of his own: his publishing company, Riot Stories, had published a volume of poetry from his old friend Dave Waller; his two record labels, Respond and Jamming, had been set up to help new musicians; he had expressed growing interest in the Campaign for Nuclear Disarmament, and had produced a TV programme about class inequality for the BBC's 'Something Else' series.

All in all, these wishes – to progress musically, to be independent and to keep his music political – had been the elements in Weller's personality and work that had made the Jam successful. But they also made it inevitable that he should eventually find it restrictive to work within the format of the group.

Above, from left: Foxton, Buckler and Weller. Right: Paul Weller with his erstwhile hero Pete Townshend.

It was during the sessions for their next album, *The Gift* (1982), that the personality clashes within the group came to a head as Weller made it clear that he thought that Rick Buckler's drumming on one track, 'Just Who Is The 5 O'Clock Hero', had destroyed the effect of the song. Only one official single was taken from the album, the double A-sided 'A Town Called Malice'/'Precious'. These songs showed Weller's preoccupation with soul music, and the single entered the charts at Number 1 in February 1982. The Jam appeared on 'Top of The Pops' on two consecutive weeks, playing both sides of the single — the first band to do so since the Beatles.

The album, which appeared the following month, also went to Number 1, Produced by Pete Wilson, *The Gift* contained some of the Jam's strongest material, notably the two tracks from the single, the album's powerful title track, the moving 'Ghosts' and a remarkable, chilling song called 'Carnation', in which Weller confronted the negative side of human nature. Trumpeter Keith Thomas and saxophone-player Steve Nichol added to the soul feel of the album.

Kicking out the Jam
For Weller, however, the Jam had outlived its useful life. His decision to disband the group became common knowledge between the release of the group's last two singles. 'The Bitterest Pill', an uncharacteristic love song, was released in September and reached Number 2, while November's 'Beat Surrender' — also released as an EP including covers of Curtis Mayfield's 'Move On Up', Edwin Starr's 'War' and the Chi-Lites' 'Stoned Out Of My Mind' alongside another Weller

original, the jazzy 'Shopping' – went to Number 1 in the wake of the split.

Weller's announcement left Bruce Foxton and Rick Buckler shocked and resentful: but Foxton embarked on a solo career, releasing two minor hit singles, 'Freak' and 'This Is The Way', in 1983, and an LP *Touch Sensitive* in 1984, while Rick Buckler formed a new band, Time UK, with former Tom Robinson Band guitarist Danny Kustow.

Paul Weller teamed up with Mick Talbot to form Style Council. Talbot had played with the Merton Parkas, the Bureau and Dexys Midnight Runners, and shared Paul's passion for soul music. Their debut single 'Speak Like A Child' made the UK Top Ten in early 1983, followed by a Top Twenty hit with the energetic 'Money Go Round'. Weller's penchant for things European was reflected in the EP *Style Council A Paris* and the 1984 debut album *Cafe Bleu*. Laced with soul and jazz sounds, the LP entered the UK album charts at Number 2. There followed a string of Top Ten singles including 'My Ever Changing Moods', 'Groovin'', 'Shout To The Top' and 'Walls Come Tumbling Down', while their second LP *Our Favourite Shop* made Number 1 in the UK in the summer of 1985. Weller kept the political edge to his lyrics while producing lilting, laid-back pop songs. He took part in the Band Aid Christmas single in 1984 and the Style Council appeared at the Live Aid concert at Wembley in 1985.

Inevitably, the Jam has to be evaluated in terms of Paul Weller's achievement alone. For all his success, he blew new life into political rock (in the widest sense) rather than took it off in any new direction. And for someone who assumed the mantle of a political spokesman, Weller never really devised a coherent political perspective. The idea he expressed in 'Trans-Global Express', that all leaders should make way for workers' co-operatives, seemed naive compared with Pete Townshend's angrier 'Meet the new boss, same as the old boss' on the Who's 1971 song 'Won't Get Fooled Again'.

At the same time, Weller remained that rare phenomenon in rock music – a man of integrity and principle, living relatively simply and using his money to help young kids and speaking honestly for a large – and often disenfranchised – section of his generation and class. It is precisely because of this commitment, which gave his songs their characteristic energy and feel, that so many of them – 'In The City', 'Eton Rifles', 'Man In The Corner Shop', 'A Town Called Malice' – will remain rock classics.   COLIN SHEARMAN

Below: Style Councillors Talbot and Weller.

THE JAM
Discography

Singles
In The City/Takin' My Love (Polydor 2058 866, 1977); All Around The World/Carnaby Street (Polydor 2058 903, 1977); The Modern World/Sweet Soul Music/Back In My Arms Again/Bricks And Mortar (Polydor 2058 945, 1977); News Of The World/Aunties And Uncles/Innocent Man (Polydor 2058 995, 1978); David Watts/"A" Bomb In Wardour Street (Polydor 2059 054, 1978); Down In The Tube Station At Midnight/So Sad About Us/The Night (Polydor POSP 8, 1978); Strange Town/Butterfly Collector (Polydor POSP 34, 1979); When You're Young/Smithers-Jones (Polydor POSP 69, 1979); Eton Rifles/See-Saw (Polydor POSP 83, 1979); Going Underground/Dreams Of Children: The Modern World/Away From The Numbers/Down In The Tube Station At Midnight (Polydor POSPJ 113, 1980); Start/Liza Radley (Polydor 2059 266, 1980); Funeral Pyre/Disguises (Polydor POSP 257, 1981); Absolute Beginners/Tales From The Riverbank (Polydor POSP 350, 1981); A Town Called Malice/Precious (Polydor POSP 400, 1982); A Town Called Malice (Live)/Precious (Polydor POSPX 400, 1982); The Bitterest Pill/Pity Poor Alfie/Fever (Polydor POSP 505, 1982); Beat Surrender/Shopping: Move On Up/Stoned Out Of My Mind/War (Polydor POSPJ 540, 1982).

Albums
In The City (Polydor 2383 447, 1977); *This Is The Modern World* (Polydor 2383 475, 1977); *All Mod Cons* (Polydor POLD 5008, 1978); *Setting Sons* (Polydor POLD 5018, 1979); *Sound Affects* (Polydor POLD 5035, 1980); *The Gift* (Polydor POLD 5055, 1982); *Dig The New Breed* (Polydor POLD 5075, 1982); *Snap!* (Polydor SNAP 1, 1983).

ALTHOUGH PUNK ROCK'S heyday is generally recalled in terms of the Sex Pistols' short but turbulent history, the Boomtown Rats must also be credited with a number of important firsts. They were, for example, the first of the 'young, loud and snotty' new-wave bands to get a single on the BBC Radio One playlist ('Looking After Number One' in August 1977), the first of their genre to achieve public acceptability without losing the staunch support of their harder-core fans, and the first successful new-wave combo to emerge from Eire.

Paths of glory

The band was formed in late 1975 as Bound for Glory, a high-speed R&B outfit whose name was stolen from the autobiography of folk singer Woody Guthrie. The group consisted of Garry Roberts (guitar and lead vocals), Johnny Fingers (keyboards), Gerry Cott (guitar), Pete Briquette (bass), Simon Crowe (drums) and Bob Geldof who, at the time, alternated between the posts of manager and lead vocalist. The son of an immigrant Belgian family who eventually worked their way up to the middle classes via a Dublin patisserie and import/export business, Geldof took a variety of jobs after leaving college, including coffee-bar manager, Spanish teacher and rock journalist in Canada. This latter enterprise was to stand him in good stead later in life when he became an arch media manipulator.

The group's *raison d'être* was familiar enough, for as Geldof later explained: '. . . there was nothing happening, Dublin being a microcosm of anywhere else. In the

The Boomtown Rats: after the goldrush

same week as we started, the Pistols started. We'd never heard of them. They'd never heard of us. But they started for essentially the same reasons, and the Ramones started in New York for the same reasons. At that time in Dublin we'd never heard of punk, but we wore what was considered to be outrageous clothing at the time . . . you know, nothing is stronger than an idea whose time has come.

'I've always said we're not a punk band, I imagine the new wave to be a line and at one end is punk and at the other is R&B-influenced rock like the Feelgoods. We're probably somewhere in between . . .'

Pest control

Despite his disclaimers, thousands of teenage punters would identify the newly re-christened Boomtown Rats as standard-bearers for the disaffected, deeply bored youth of the nation. In 1977, the band were signed to Ensign Records and moved to London, where they were able to reach a large, impressionable audience with their melodic, but definitely angst-ridden songs. They quickly established themselves as a top-line new-wave act with their first album, *The Boomtown Rats* (written and rehearsed before they ever left Ireland) which was released in August 1977 and reached Number 18 in the UK charts.

The album afforded hit singles in the speedy R&B and punk overtones of 'Looking After Number One' (Number 11) and 'Mary Of The Fourth Form' (Number 15) but it was with their second album, *A Tonic For The Troops*, released in June 1978, that the band truly made their mark. This reached Number 8 and remained on the LP charts in the UK for 44 weeks, while 'Rat Trap', a single which told of the familiar hopelessness of life in an urban wasteland, made the Number 1 position in the UK in November of that year.

Above: King Rat Bob Geldof, the band's vociferous spokesman, relaxes in luxurious surroundings. Like several other bands, the Rats took their name from a book by William Burroughs.

Cash and controversy

Like the Pistols, Clash *et al*, the Rats' history was rich in controversy. They were banned from playing a triumphant home-coming gig at Dublin's Leopardstown race-course, local authorities fearing riots and public insurrection, they had a major disagreement with their record label over claimed unpaid royalties which delayed the release of their third album, *The Fine Art Of Surfacing* (1979), and their best-known single, 'I Don't Like Mondays' was

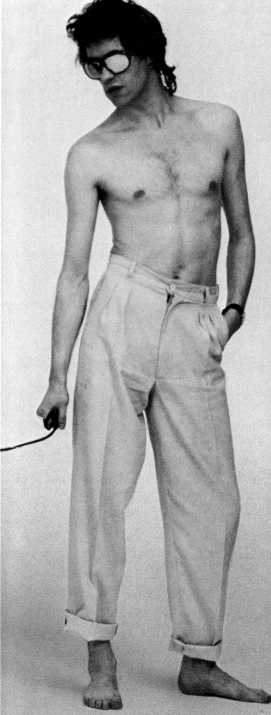

Far left: The Boomtown Rats caged! Left: Singer Bob Geldof flanked by bassist Pete Briquette (right) and guitarist Gerry Cott. Below: Rat with friendly cat.

not only banned by many American radio stations but also cited as prejudicial to the defence of the teenage girl whose brief moment of infamy it chronicled.

'Mondays' was Geldof's commentary on a strange and horrific event that took place earlier that year in Santa Ana, California. 16-year-old Brenda Spencer had barri-caded herself in a house opposite her school playground. When the school gates opened that morning, she used her father's gun to wound eight of her school chums and kill the headmaster and school janitor, her only explanation being, 'I don't like Mondays – this livens up the day.'

As a piece of social comment, 'Mondays' was certainly astute, but it also proved that eloquence, melody and intelligent arrangements had found their way back into protest music. In 1979 most of the Rats' contemporaries – those still intact, that is – were still thrashing out the same old amphetamine-driven cliches.

In 1979 the Boomtown Rats embarked on an ambitious world tour, taking in markets as diverse as Japan, Canada and Thailand. Although their American fortunes never really took off in the wake of the Brenda Spencer débâcle, they still maintained a loyal following there among hard-core Anglophiles. And even if they failed to understand a word of the band's musical messages, foreign audiences were easily bowled over by the sheer pace and ebullience of their live gigs.

Johnny Fingers brought a rare flamboy-ance to the keyboards and used the unlikely gambit of wearing pyjamas (on *and* off-stage) and dancing all over the place. Guitarists Pete Briquette and Gerry Cott were every bit as innervating as the most energetic punk strummers of the era *and* could play considerably more than three chords. Stage front, Geldof would strut, cavort, cajole and, of course, sing – in tune! Thus, with the regular addition of tenor sax-player Dave McHale (who re-created the raucous playing that had featured on 'Rat Trap'), the band were able to reproduce their increasingly ambitious recorded arrangements on stage with considerable accuracy.

The material world

Although Bob Geldof was always very much the focal point of the band, the other group members had vital roles to play, even though they might have lacked Geldof's reserves of charisma. Both Crowe and Briquette, for example, were essential to the appeal of the Rats's arrangements, and were also quite able and willing to articulate policy, musical or otherwise. Crowe explained the Rats' philosophy in a 1980 interview, saying that '. . . we want to be around for a while – if we'd produced another "Mondays" or "Rat Trap", we could've done that, but we don't need to.' Crowe went on to say that the band found it more exciting to take risks.

However, Geldof himself admitted that 'I want money because it will buy me individual freedom. It's a materialistic world [and] this world constricts me . . . I don't like it, I just want totally out of this society and the only way I can see out is to have more money than anyone else, to give me choices, options.' Geldof was aware of the danger of using politically loaded lyrics in order to make his pile. 'The crucial point,' he told one reporter, 'is I genuinely don't want to feel that I've got anything to preach or that the band has anything to teach. We're not presumptuous enough to dare to tell people how to run their lives. I don't want kids to come to a political rally when they come to the Rats. I think all revolutions are meaningless, especially ones led by CBS and EMI.'

Coming up for air

1980 found the Boomtown Rats maintain-ing a high level of popularity. The year's two singles, 'Someone's Looking At You' and the reggae-tinged 'Banana Republic', both made the UK Top Five, while *The Fine Art Of Surfacing*, released the pre-vious October, stayed on the charts for 26 weeks, peaking at Number 7. But by this time, Geldof's glib wisdom, ready wit and endearing brogue had established him as the darling of the chat-show circuit and the gossip columns and his very status as a media figure now began to turn many fans away from the band. 1981's *Mondo Bongo* album reached Number 6 but stayed in the charts a mere seven weeks, while 'The Elephant's Graveyard (Guilty)' only reached Number 26 in the singles charts.

The group toured sporadically but audiences dwindled and, with the depar-ture of Gerry Cott in 1981 and Geldof further denting his credibility by taking the lead role in Alan Parker's film of the Pink Floyd's *The Wall*, the Rats' ship appeared to be slowly sinking. Somewhat predictably, the music press revelled in the Boomtown Rats' decline. *Mondo Bongo*, admittedly a rather tepid album, received less than favourable reviews – 'There's a helluva lot of depth, decision and *emotion* missing from what is one of the most self-indulgent pop scenarios of late,' com-mented *Sounds* – while its 1982 follow up, *V Deep*, only managed to scrape to Number 64 in the LP chart.

Geldof's own solo debut, *Deep In The Heart Of Nowhere* signalled the Rats' split, yet fared even worse chartwise at Number 79. More important, though, was his lead-ing role in Band Aid and its Live Aid spin-off that saved countless lives in famine-struck Ethiopia. The award of an honorary knight-hood followed (as an Eire citizen, he could not be 'Sir Bob'), while his marriage to wri-ter and media personality Paula Yates ensured he would remain in the spotlight, whatever his musical future. MARK WILLIAMS

Boomtown Rats
Recommended Listening
The Fine Art Of Surfacing (Ensign ENROX 11)
(Includes: When The Night Comes, Wind Chill Factor (Minus Zero), Keep It Up, I Don't Like Mondays, Someone's Looking, Diamond Smiles).

TALK OF THE TOWN

In January 1980, the Pretenders had every reason to feel pleased with themselves. Their debut album had just waltzed into the UK LP charts at Number 1; simultaneously, their third single, 'Brass In Pocket', was staring down at the competition from the top of the singles listings. Three years later, two of them were dead and the future careers of the two survivors looked uncertain.

Mystery achievement
Ever since Chrissie Hynde left the US for London in the summer of 1973, she had been broke, homeless and planning to form a band.

Born in Akron, Ohio, on 7 September 1951, in the bleak American Midwest, Chrissie had grown up with the radio on, and tuned into the Beatles, the Rolling

How the Pretenders paid the price of success

Stones and the Kinks. Even as a child, she had wanted nothing more than an electric guitar in her hands and a stage to play it on: the first group she formed was Sat Sun Mat, which also featured Mark Mothersbaugh, later to resurface with Devo. Graduating from Kent State University with a degree in fine art, her ambitions drew her eventually to London.

A series of chance encounters led to a brief engagement as a writer with *New Musical Express*; she then worked as an assistant at Sex, a King's Road clothes shop run by Vivienne Westwood and Malcolm McLaren. Chrissie then returned to Ohio, appearing with Jack Rabbit, a

Cleveland bar band, before travelling to Paris to sing in the Frenchies, managed by an acquaintance of hers, Marc Zermati. Six months later, the band split: after several abortive attempts to form a new group, Chrissie decided to head back to London.

A Real recruit
In the summer of 1975, the first strategies for the eventual punk revolution of 1977 were being mapped out by Malcolm McLaren and an assorted gang of would-be musical activists. Having been introduced to this circle when working for McLaren at Sex, Chrissie was soon rehearsing with a variety of intriguing line-ups.

In March 1978, she met Dave Hill, who had just formed his own record label, Real. He signed her up and decided to bankroll her while she continued her search for the musicians who might spark her songs into vivid life. One of them proved to be Pete Farndon, who had spent the previous year playing bass in an Australian country-rock band called the Bushwackers. For a short time he and Chrissie were lovers, and he helped her organise her group. Chrissie had already found a drummer named Gerry Mackleduff; Pete decided that he was adequate for the job but that they needed a guitarist.

Farndon enlisted James Honeyman Scott, whom he remembered from his native Hereford. They recorded demo versions of Chrissie's 'Precious' and 'Phone Call' and the Kinks' 'Stop Your Sobbing'. Hynde then took the tapes to Nick Lowe, who agreed to produce the Pretenders' first single. Working quickly in studio time donated by Elvis Costello (who was then recording *Armed Forces* with Lowe), he fashioned versions of 'Stop Your Sobbing' and 'The Wait' (a Hynde-Farndon original) that surpassed the expectations even of Chrissie's staunchest supporters.

By now, Martin Chambers, another of Farndon's Hereford connections, had replaced Mackleduff on drums. The Pretenders were thus ready for their first headlining gigs: they played the Moonlight Club in West Hampstead in January 1979. Within weeks, they were on the cover of *Melody Maker*, thanks to a powerful publicity campaign organised by Real's parent company, WEA. However, 'Stop Your Sobbing' was not quite the hit that most critics had predicted, only reaching Number 34. In June the Pretenders released 'Kid', a glorious lament with a vocal performance by Chrissie that seemed capable of melting the sternest heart; it also floundered short of the Top Thirty.

Leading the field
The band at last broke through with the October release of 'Brass In Pocket', an audacious, irresistible piece of self-promotion that seemed to sound better with every play; by January 1980 it was Number 1. The Pretenders cunningly delayed the release of their first LP until the new year, *Pretenders* thus becoming the first Number 1 album of the Eighties.

The Pretenders had a number of advantages over their punk contemporaries that helped to ensure them mass acceptance. Their strong melodies and jangly guitars evoked the golden days of the Sixties beat groups, while Chrissie's passionate singing recalled Dusty Springfield in its mixture of power and vulnerability. These familiar elements were harnessed to a distinctly modern urgency and attack.

But as Europe and America fell under heir spell, the Pretenders became intoxicated by their sudden success, acquiring a reputation for excess: alcohol and narcotics seemed to provide powerful antidotes to the exhausting tours the band embarked upon. Hynde's creative muse, too, was having problems. During 1980, the Pretenders released only one new tune, 'Talk Of The Town'. A year later they put out

Opposite: Chrissie Hynde, whose forceful songwriting, singing and playing helped put brass in the Pretenders' pockets. Above: The band on stage, from left Farndon, Hynde, Chambers and Honeyman Scott.

'Message Of Love', which prefaced their second LP, *Pretenders II*.

Released in August 1981, the album was virtually laughed out of town. A darker, more sombre record than its predecessor, its harshness had been dictated by the group's reactions to their success, their growing disenchantment with its attendant pressures and an increasingly compli-

> 'You work so hard for two years to get into a position where you're allowed to make records and get paid for it. And a lot of people really blow it. You've *got* to keep the thing ticking over, you've gotta nurture it like it's something that's alive. You can't leave it for too long or it'll seize up and die . . . Sometimes you can't start over.'
> **Chrissie Hynde**, 1983

cated pattern of personal relationships within the band. The music press hated the LP, especially in Britain, and the band's pleasure at its eventual commercial success (and that of a single taken from it, a fine cover of Ray Davies' 'I Go To Sleep' that made Number 7 in the UK), must have been soured by the critical drubbing.

However, the band suffered a far more serious setback when, eight weeks into their US tour, Martin Chambers injured his arm and hand after punching a glass lampshade. The tour had to be postponed, losing them precious momentum and profits. The Pretenders completed their remaining US dates and a world tour by mid 1982, but further unhappiness and tragedy were waiting in the wings. On 14 June, Pete Farndon was sacked, the group claiming that his behaviour had been hopelessly erratic and unreliable. Two days later, James Honeyman Scott was found dead in a friend's flat in West

London. The cause of death was attributed to a deadly cocktail of alcohol and cocaine.

Chrissie Hynde and Martin Chambers decided to battle on, recording 'Back On The Chain Gang' with ex-Rockpile guitarist Billy Bremner and bassist Tony Butler, who later joined Big Country. A Number 17 hit in the UK, its success did little to dispel the melancholic atmosphere surrounding the band. Ignoring widespread speculation about their future, Hynde and Chambers busied themselves with finding replacement members. Robbie McIntosh, formerly of Night and Manfred Mann's Earth Band, was recruited on guitar, while Malcolm Foster, previously a Foster Brother, was hired as bass player.

Learning to crawl
In April 1983 Pete Farndon died, killed by a lethal mixture of heroin and cocaine. Although he was no longer part of the group, the death of one who had done so much to realise Chrissie Hynde's musical vision intensified the aura of tragedy that now hung around the group.

After the release of 'Back On The Chain Gang' in September 1982, little was heard from the Pretenders. Chrissie had a child in January 1983 by her former hero, now boyfriend, Ray Davies of the Kinks, and then went back into the studio to record an LP, *Learning To Crawl*, which included the 1983 Christmas hit '2000 Miles'.

With the departure of Martin Chambers for 1986's *Get Close,* The Pretenders were down to Chrissie Hynde and a cast of supporting players. She broke up with Davies, married Simple Minds' Jim Kerr, had another child and even found time to guest on one-time support band UB40's hit singles. Hynde has finally, it seemed, found happiness.
ALLAN JONES

Pretenders
Recommended Listening
Pretenders (Real RAL 3) (Includes: Brass In Pocket, Mystery Achievement, Lovers Of Today, Up The Neck, Kid, The Phone Call); *Pretenders II* (Real K 56924) (Includes: Louie Louie, Pack It Up, Bad Boys Get Spanked, Talk Of The Town, Jealous Dogs, Day After Day).

Look Sharp!

The maverick style of Joe Jackson

FROM 'SPIV-ROCKER' to the 'acceptable face of punk', from 'Forties Hep Cat' to sophisticated champagne-and-taxi crooner, Joe Jackson had about as many musical identities as he had watches in his coat on the cover of his second LP, *I'm The Man* (1979). But Jackson was no dilettante, with one ear to the fashion scene and the other to the charts. Instead, the different musical styles that he explored represented expressions of his eclectic taste, and he proved to be one of the most durable artists to emerge from the new wave.

Wide-eyed and legless

Jackson had always been an outsider. Born in Burton-on-Trent in 1955 but raised in Portsmouth, he was an awkward and gawky kid, who suffered from asthma. 'I was a slightly odd teenager,' he once recalled. 'A normal teenager goes to youth clubs and tries desperately to pick up girls and plays football. I didn't do those things.'

As with many adolescent misfits, Jackson turned to music for comfort and solace: he taught himself to play the piano, and at 16 began his formal musical training at the Royal Academy of Music. Although he was rated as a highly promising concert pianist, Jackson was never sure about what he wanted to do until, after three years at the Academy, he turned to rock.

One of his first groups, Edward Bear, was a 'shameless pop band' whose demise led to the formation, in 1974, of Jackson's first major foray into rock, Arms and Legs. The band released three singles but soon broke up due to mismanagement and lack of record-company support. Bassist Graham Maby was to remain a stalwart of Jackson's subsequent bands.

After the failure of Arms and Legs, Jackson returned to Portsmouth where he worked for nine months playing piano at the local Playboy Club. After quitting that job, he spent six months on the road with a cabaret act called Coffee and Cream. But this was 1977, and when Jackson heard bands like the Clash and the Damned, decided to try rock again.

Jackson had been careful with his money and so was able to finance a series of demos, which he pressed into album form. He made the rounds of the record companies and was soundly rejected by them all, but was advised by United Artists to get in touch with Albion Music, a publishing company. John Telfer, who later became Jackson's manager, signed him to a publishing deal and sent his demo to A&M producer David Kershenbaum. Jackson and his band – Maby, Gary Sanford (guitar) and Dave Houghton (drums) – were in the studio with Kershenbaum before a contract was even signed.

Left: Joe introduces 'Sunday Papers', a song from his first LP that poured scorn on the tabloid press.

Recorded live – Jackson claimed there were no overdubs – *Look Sharp!* was completed in a week and a half and was released in February 1979 to unanimously positive reviews. *Rolling Stone* called it 'a stripped-down paean to spontaneous combustion'. Certainly its songs – the Number 13 UK hit 'Is She Really Going Out With Him?', 'Look Sharp' and 'Fools In Love' – with their quirky rhythms, searing guitar riffs and intelligently ironic lyrics were evidence of a unique musical persona, the streetwise neurotic.

After the release of *Look Sharp!*, and its subsequent success on both sides of the Atlantic, Jackson began expounding his idea of 'spiv rock' in order to poke fun at musical categorising. 'I think people always want to put a label on what you do, so I thought I'd be one step ahead of them and invent one myself,' Jackson said years later. He took the idea a step further on his second album, *I'm The Man*, posing on the cover as a spiv – with a polka-dot tie and pencil moustache – selling stolen watches.

I'm The Man contained the same stripped-down pop sound and biting lyrics of the debut album, and was even more successful. Released in the autumn of 1979, it reached Number 12 in the British LP charts, gave Jackson his first Top Ten hit in the UK, 'It's Different For Girls', and firmly established him in the US as one of the stars of the new wave. The highlight of the album was 'On The Radio'; frenetic, but still melodic, this was a triumphant act of revenge. As Jackson put it: 'It's addressed to all the teachers, all the bullies, all the people who wouldn't listen before.'

Jiving with Joe

But Jackson's success brought difficulties. The fickle rock press was turning against him, and at London's Dingwalls he was hit on the head with a bottle by a member of the audience. 'I don't really fit in,' confessed Joe at the time. 'I look a bit odd and I'm easy to take the piss out of because I'm six foot two and I'm going bald.' Because Jackson was feeling increasingly at odds with the rock world, he turned to reggae, releasing a cover version of Jimmy Cliff's 'The Harder They Come' in 1980, and playing keyboards for reggae band the Rasses on three tracks of their *Natural Wild* LP.

His own band's next album, *Beat Crazy*, released in October 1980, also reflected his interest in reggae; highly rhythmic and percussive, it took critics off-guard and, perhaps not surprisingly, was not as successful as the previous offerings. The LP reflected Jackson's uneasiness with conventional pop music and his disillusionment with rock – his liner notes read: '. . . we knew it was destined to failure . . . why did we try?'

Jackson's next project turned out to be even less predictable than *Beat Crazy*; *Jumpin' Jive*, released in the summer of 1981, was a collection of Forties swing standards and although Jackson could not hope to capture the spontaneity and virtuosity of Cab Calloway, Louis Jordan

and other 'hep cats', the album displayed his piano skills to good advantage and showed a rich electicism of musical interests. The album was a surprise hit in the UK, reaching Number 14.

New York nights

Following *Jumpin' Jive*, Jackson spent a year in New York, immersing himself in the wide variety of its nightlife and listening to the array of ethnic music that can be found only in that city. The result was Jackson's most successful album, *Night And Day*, released in June 1982. The LP was divided into two parts: the 'Day' side was filled with slow, lush ballads, reflecting a new introspective romanticism. The 'Night' side, meanwhile, was made up of dance music – salsa, R&B, rock, the kind of music to be heard daily on the streets of New York.

Night And Day was an enormous success, particularly in the US, and afforded another hit single in 'Steppin' Out', which reached Number 6 in both the US and UK charts. The album reflected a new maturity; Joe had obviously taken all the myriad styles of music that appealed to him and, instead of aping them as he had in his transitional period, synthesised them into something distinctive and personal.

Above: Bassist Graham Maby joins Joe on the stand. Below: The artist 'feels a song coming on . . .'

From June 1982 to May 1983, Jackson and his new band toured the world to promote *Night And Day*. Between two legs of the tour, Jackson wrote the score to *Mike's Murder*, an off-beat murder movie set against a backdrop of the druggy punk underworld, and the soundtrack album was another success, reaching the American Top Thirty. Joe's 1984 LP *Body And Soul* added the acoustics of an ancient Masonic Lodge hall to the rich variety of songs.

Jackson's deliberate eclecticism—a three-sided live set, *Big World,* in 1986, an instrumental LP, *Will Power,* in 1987, another soundtrack, *Tucker,* in 1988—lost him a commercial following. But at least no-one was sticking labels on him anymore.   DEBBIE GELLER

Joe Jackson
Recommended Listening
Look Sharp! (A&M AMID 120) (Includes: Sunday Papers, One More Time, Throw It Away, Is She Really Going Out With Him?, Pretty Girls, Look Sharp!); *Night And Day* (A&M AMLH 64906) (Includes: Cancer, Steppin' Out, Real Men, Chinatown, Another World, Target).

SQUEEZE

An East Side Story of pop promise

IN THEIR TIME, Squeeze were a group that epitomised the misfit; they never slotted neatly into any particular category, fashion or movement. Indeed, their records, especially towards the end of their career, displayed a diversity of style that few groups could equal. They were, in short, a classic pop group, boasting as they did the ingenious songwriting team of Glenn Tilbrook and Chris Difford whose songs allied catchy melodies and hooklines with clever, graphic lyrics and won them from some quarters the unwanted accolade of 'the second Lennon and McCartney'.

Despite the independence of Squeeze's vision and stance, they acquired, at the beginning of their recording career, an association with the punk/new-wave movement of 1976-77. Their debut recording, a three-song EP on Miles Copeland's Deptford Fun City label entitled *Packet Of*

Three, appeared in the independent racks in 1977. The content of the record, particularly 'Cat On A Wall', was vaguely consistent with the punk style, but the musicianship displayed indicated that the group were no typical garage-band-made-good. In fact, they had been together for a number of years; Difford, Tilbrook, bassist Harry Kakoulli and Jools Holland, an accomplished boogie-woogie style pianist, were old schoolfriends from Deptford in South-east London; drummer Gilson Lavis, who completed the band, was a seasoned session man who had toured with Chuck Berry and other visiting US artists.

Punks in the disco

They were a motley crew; the angelic Tilbrook sung in a light, melodic style that complemented his looks and played slick, fluid lead guitar, while lyricist Difford

Below: Guitarists Chris Difford (left) and Glenn Tilbrook (centre) on stage with the band's first bassist Harry Kakoulli.

looked and sounded rougher, playing scratchy, churning rhythm guitar and singing in a gruff, low-pitched, deadpan style. Holland, invariably dressed in sharp suit and a selection of colourful ties, came over as the archetypal wide-boy complete with shades, huge cigar and fast-talking stage raps. Kakoulli, with shoulder-length hair, and the powerfully-built Lavis completed a visual image that defied stereotyping. Squeeze's first single after signing to the major A&M label, 'Take Me I'm Yours', was a complete break from punk, sung in octave unison by Tilbrook and Difford against a disco beat and Holland's swirling synthesisers. It was a hit, making Number 19 in the UK charts, but the follow-up, 'Bang Bang', flopped.

Ex-Velvet Underground bass player John Cale produced the group's debut album, *Squeeze* (1978), and his influence was evident in the stark arrangements of songs like 'Out Of Control', an edgy slice of hard-rock with schoolboy-smut lyrics. This initiated accusations of sexism that took a

long time for Squeeze to shake off. The title track of their second LP *Cool For Cats* (1979), produced by John Wood, along with the likes of 'Slap And Tickle', 'It's Not Cricket' and the ambiguous 'It's So Dirty' (actually a put-down of sexist attitudes) continued Difford's obsession with nights out with the lads looking for birds and booze. 'Cool For Cats' and 'Up The Junction' both made Number 2 in the UK charts, the latter a sad tale of young marriage doomed to failure sung by Tilbrook to one of his most enchanting melodies. 'Slap And Tickle' also made Number 24 when released as a single, confirming Squeeze's new-found popularity as pop's heirs to Ian Dury's Cockney crown.

In 1980, *Argybargy* saw them developing towards a wider variety of styles such as the mini-opera of 'Separate Beds' the full-blooded pop of 'Pulling Mussels From A Shell' and the swing of 'Wrong Side Of The Moon', written by Holland and Difford and sung by the former. With 'I Think I'm Go-Go' Difford and Tilbrook succeeded in conveying the automaton-like aspects of the pop-star existence without falling into self-indulgence, singing a verse each with appropriate backing textures to suit their contrasting voices. The album saw the debut of John Bentley on bass after Harry Kakoulli had departed, later to resurface with ex-Dart John Dummer in the outrageous True Life Confessions.

Down the Tube

After extensive touring as far afield as Australia, Squeeze also lost Jools Holland; he had begun to contribute songs to the group's records, as well as cutting his own discs on Deptford Fun City, and was looking for an outlet for his considerable piano talents, which had essentially been underused by the group. He formed his own group, the Millionaires, but later found greater success as a television personality, utilising the quick-witted humour that had been an important part of Squeeze's live act as host of 'The Tube'.

Meanwhile, Squeeze hit more turmoil when they forsook Copeland's management in favour of Jake Riviera, who subsequently released them. The association did, however, lead to the recruitment of Ace keyboardist Paul Carrack, who had written that group's only hit single 'How Long?'. Under the production team of Elvis Costello and Roger Bechirian, they went into the studio to record *East Side Story* (1981), an album that was to prove the ultimate example of their supreme pop craftsmanship.

From the standard Squeeze pop fare of 'In Quintessence' and 'Is That Love' to the rockabilly of 'Messed Around', *East Side Story* used a wider than ever range of musical settings for Difford's increasingly eloquent lyrics. 'Vanity Fair' saw Tilbrook's tender vocal set against an orchestra, while 'Someone Else's Heart' showed Difford adopting a softer, more sensitive delivery than he had previously

Top: Squeeze's late-Seventies line-up, from left Difford, Jools Holland, Tilbrook, Gilson Lavis and John Bentley. Above: Holland bids the band farewell at the Albany, Deptford, in August 1980.

attempted. 'Labelled With Love' saw Tilbrook demonstrate how to sing a country and western song with an English accent and gave the group a UK Number 4 hit single, while 'Tempted', which saw Carrack in superb voice, provided the band with their first Stateside success.

A new label

Carrack then left and was replaced by Don Snow, who played on the LP *Sweets For A Stranger* (1982), on which Elvis Costello and Paul Young added vocals to the single 'Black Coffee In Bed'. Although the LP was considered a Squeeze classic, the album's sales failed to match those of the band's earlier releases, and Squeeze decided to call it a day. Their 'greatest hits' compilation LP *Singles – 45's And Under* (1982) subsequently made Number 3 in the UK album charts. Difford and Tilbrook went on to start a project with various session players and recorded the LP *Difford And Tilbrook* before disbanding in

1984. Their songs had featured in the musical *Labelled With Love* at Deptford's Albany Empire, where Tilbrook became a regular DJ. Lavis joined Graham Parker for the 1983 album *The Real Macaw*.

After a one-off gig at a pub in Catford, south London, in early 1985, Squeeze decided to reform with the original line-up, plus Keith Wilkinson. The band received a rapturous reception as special guests of U2 before a crowd of 80,000 in Dublin.

The unfailing quality of Squeeze was evident on their LP *Cosi Fan Tutti Frutti* released in 1985. Two years later, *Babylon And On* reverted to the cheery Cockney singalongs of old and spawned a UK Top Ten hit in 'Hourglass' with second keyboardist Andy Metcalfe swelling the ranks. JOHN VOYSEY

Squeeze
Recommended Listening

Cool For Cats (A&M AMLH 68503) (Includes: Cool For Cats, The Knack, Up The Junction, Slap And Tickle, Slightly Drunk, Revue); *East Side Story* (A&M AMLH 64854) (Includes: Messed Around, Someone Else's Heart, Tempted, Piccadilly, Mumbo Jumbo, Labelled With Love).

YESTERDAY ONCE MORE

How Eighties pop echoed the hits of the past

IN THE EIGHTIES, mass unemployment returned to the UK for the first time in half a century. Rock, ever reflective of the mood of the times, accompanied the economy into recession.

Pretty but dumb
Ever since the mid Seventies, there had been indications that rock was coming full circle. Groups like Dr Feelgood had tried to break away from what was perceived as its increasing pretentiousness and emasculation by returning to the straightforward, hard-hitting style of late-Fifties rock 'n'roll. Their albums comprised short, high-energy songs while their appearance – short hair, together with ties, jackets and narrow-bottomed trousers – similarly rejected the prevailing styles of the day (loon pants and long hair) to embrace the fashions of the Fifties. The punk movement consolidated this change of emphasis by going back to the beginnings of rock

The songs of such Fifties stars as Perry Como (top) were revived by Eighties bands like the Jets (above).

'n'roll in the mid Fifties to rediscover its raucous, fiery verve.

By the Eighties, these links with the Fifties had strengthened. The most obvious factor was that popular music was, once more, 'pop'. In the late Sixties 'pop' had evolved into 'rock', but by the Eighties it had resumed its former character. Rock music had always harboured artistic or intellectual pretensions, however spurious. Pop had none – it was fun, immediate and innocuous. Its re-emergence could be attributed to the fact that rock had reached a cul-de-sac and that it simply seemed time for a change.

Its revival could also be explained by the harsh economic situation. The high-mindedness of rock suddenly became out of place as young people understandably felt the need for music of a purely escapist nature.

At the same time, the amount of money teenagers had to spend on records had fallen; they could no longer afford expensive LPs and so purchased singles instead. Record companies, faced with declining revenue, reacted by raising the prices of albums, thereby providing even less of an incentive to buy them; the single once more became the predominant artefact of popular music.

Singles were obviously designed to have an immediate impact on the listener; this meant that bands concentrated on achieving an attractive overall sound rather than on musical or lyrical subtlety. Lyrics, in particular, diminished in importance; most fans did not buy Duran Duran's records for the wisdom of their words. Culture Club's 'I'll Tumble 4 Ya' exemplified the subordinate role of lyrics in the new pop music; the song virtually consisted of a repetition of the title phrase.

In the early and mid Fifties, some of the lyrics of rock'n'roll songs (such as those by Chuck Berry and Leiber and Stoller) had been very clever, but by the end of the deade they had become more functional and less interesting.

Picture pop
As the economic recession helped make pop commercially and aesthetically attractive once more, a pop star's appearance became as important as his or her music – recalling the Fifties, when the faces of film stars had launched a thousand glossy magazines. Early rock performers, often regarded as poor man's movie stars, had been marketed in a similar way. In the Eighties the pattern was re-established; if anything, a performer's photogenic qualities took precedence over his musical abilities.

Reflecting this trend, the Eighties saw a resurgence of the type of magazine that relied for its appeal as much on pictorial as on journalistic quality. The groundbreaker in this respect was *Smash Hits*, launched by Nick Logan, which made liberal use of photographs and adopted an easy-to-read presentation. Within three years it had overtaken *New Musical Express* as the UK's leading popular music

The late-Seventies rockabilly revival was fuelled by the style of John Travolta in Grease (above) and the Stray Cats' guitarist Brian Setzer (right).

publication. While the circulations of the traditional rock weeklies went into what appeared to be an irreversible decline, those of the 'photo mags' began to soar. Having seen which way the cookie was crumbling, *Record Mirror* transformed itself from a tabloid newspaper to a small, glossy magazine format.

Nick Logan then moved from *Smash Hits* to start the *Face*, a magazine whose very title emphasised that style was the name of the rock game in the Eighties. This attitude was reminiscent of the Fifties, but the parallels extended in many cases to the actual fashions that were featured in the *Face*'s pages.

There are those who will claim that the James Dean/Marlon Brando persona had never been out of fashion, but in the Eighties it was right back in vogue, having been re-popularised primarily by John Travolta in the 1978 movie *Grease*. The leather-jacketed rocker image was later adopted by groups as diverse as punk-rockers the Clash and teen-heroes Wham!

Only rock'n'roll?

With the whole nature of the pop market increasingly assuming characteristics of the Fifties, it was only to be expected that there would be straightforward musical links between the two periods. Most notably, there were the Stray Cats, a three-man group whose leader, Brian Setzer, was obsessed with the pop icons of the Fifties. With Jim McDonnell and Lee 'Rocker' Drucker, he formed a group committed to playing the kind of rockabilly music that had been neglected since the passing of the Fifties. The Stray Cats took their musical stance from such artists as Carl Perkins and Johnny Burnette and, with their leather gear and extravagant greaser hairstyles, captured the look of, as well as sounded like, those vintage Fifties performers.

They built a reputation playing clubs in the UK, and purveyed such an authentic sound that they came to the attention of rock'n'roll devotee Dave Edmunds. He produced their debut album, *The Stray Cats* (1981), which attracted considerable attention and provided UK hit singles in 'Runaway Boys', 'Stray Cat Strut' and 'Rock This Town'.

In the final analysis, however, their success was solid but not spectacular in the UK; in the US, they took off in sensational style after being the support band on the Rolling Stones' 1981 US tour. It seemed strange that a group so obviously time-lagged should suddenly become so fashionable; but their voguishness was proved beyond doubt by the fact that McDonnell became engaged to film star Britt Ekland, who had hovered at or near the vortex of rock fashion since the early Seventies, notably as the girlfriend of Rod Stewart.

The tactic of recreating the Fifties also paid off handsomely for Shakin' Stevens. It was perhaps significant that he had been performing as a rock revivalist for at least 10 years, but it was only in the early

Above: Mari Wilson in full Fifties regalia, complete with 'bee-hive' hairdo. Below: Shakin' Stevens – Wales' Eighties answer to Elvis Presley.

Eighties that he shot to stardom. Then there was Bananarama, who represented a mini-revival of the all-girl vocal trio, a particularly popular style of the Fifties and Sixties. Bananarama's 1983 hit 'Cruel Summer' returned to the adolescent pre-occupations of that period that had been reflected in such contemporary songs as Carole King's 'It Might As Well Rain Until September'.

Revival of the fittest

Several songs from the pre-Beatle period of rock were also successfully revived; Shirley Ellis' 'The Clapping Song' became a hit for all-girl group the Belle Stars, while Mari Wilson successfully covered Julie London's 'Cry Me A River'. It suddenly became fashionable to plunder a store of Fifties and early Sixties recordings that had hitherto been thought of as hopelessly 'uncool' by rock artists: Modern Romance had a Top Ten hit with 'Cherry Pink And Apple Blossom White', a major 1955 hit for trumpeter Eddie Calvert; rockabilly revivalists the Jets had a minor hit with an engaging rendition of a Perry Como song, 'Love Makes The World Go Round'; the Piranhas revived the South African *kwela* 'Tom Hark', and Tight Fit had a Number 1 hit with The Tokens' 'The Lion Sleeps Tonight'. Shakin' Stevens himself, though closely modelling himself on Elvis Presley, delved further back for two of his major hits, Rosemary Clooney's 1955 hit 'This Ole House' and 'Green Door', a US Number 1 for Jim Lowe a quarter of a century earlier in 1956.

Swinging again

As Fifties styles began to lose some of their novelty value by the early Eighties, those of the Sixties also came into vogue in the UK. Sixties nostalgia was fuelled by the re-running of hit TV series such as 'The Avengers', 'The Prisoner' and 'Rowan And Martin's Laugh-In'. Record companies took note of the new trend, re-releasing LPs by Sixties artists ranging from the Kinks and Manfred Mann to Scott Walker and Honor Blackman. Stars as diverse as Billy Joel, Siouxsie and the Banshees and Tracey Ullman all profited by cashing in on Sixties musical fashions.

While jaded cynics might scoff at the lack of so-called 'original' ideas that pop music seemed to offer in the Eighties, there was no denying the exciting variety of images and musical styles on show, with artists rummaging through the fashions of bygone eras – whether rock'n'roll, acid rock or glam-rock – in a mad free-for-all.

BOB WOFFINDEN

Hicks from the Sticks

The Sex Pistols' Anarchy Tour sparked off a regional rock revolution

WITH THE BENEFIT of hindsight – and several years of opinionated documentation – it is clear that the arrival of the Sex Pistols' Anarchy Tour at Leeds Polytechnic on 7 December 1976 was the preface to a peculiarly provincial story. Although the Pistols' supposed effects on the established record industry were the subject of media overkill, one aspect of their influence was less widely known; that concert started the process of UK rock's decentralisation away from London.

All the Sex Pistols' previous provincial shows had been cancelled by councils intimidated by the band's growing notoriety in the wake of their Bill Grundy TV interview on 1 December; Leeds thus became the first date of the Anarchy Tour. It was here that the future members of Soft Cell, (Southern) Death Cult, Danse Society *et al* got their first crucial fix on the Pistols' 'anyone can play' principle; here that the jaded anti-establishment at last found fresh and irresistible new heroes in the Pistols and support acts the Clash, the Jam and the Damned; here that future promoters, independent label entrepreneurs and still-amateur rock cognoscenti were first seduced into considering that rock 'n'roll could be their future too.

Jerks and Squares

The Anarchy Tour subsequently hit other northern cities, where its impact appeared to produce further results. It was against this background – and as a direct result of its inspiration – that new northern bands began to form, proliferate and even flourish in the years that followed. In the immediate aftermath of the Pistols' gig, new outfits mushroomed all over Leeds and West Yorkshire. SOS (later to metamorphose into Girls At Our Best), the all-girl four-piece the Straits, the Jerks (briefly with Lightning Records) and the Squares all flourished for some time, although only the last-named of these got even close to breaking through, signing with Sire Records after the company's president, Seymour Stein, heard their debut, self-produced, record on John Peel's Radio One show.

The Gang of Four – first famed in Leeds for an extravagant punk version of Dylan's 'A Hard Rain's A-Gonna Fall' that they usually included in their set – and the Mekons were the first bands to win more than local attention. In time, there developed a healthy rivalry between these and Cabaret Voltaire and the Human League in nearby Sheffield. In general, however, all the odds were heavily stacked against provincial bands, mostly because the UK record industry and rock media were London-based. As a result, their writers and A&R people were unable either to follow or to understand what was happening in regional

centres of activity like Leeds.

A persistent problem, and one that continued into the Eighties, was that the rock press was staffed almost exclusively by London journalists, while the provincials they did hire invariably moved to London and were thus unable adequately to stay in touch with new regional developments. The new freelancers working for the music press who actually remained in the provinces operated as token outposts, never being given the authority personally to 'discover' a new band. Editorial policy-makers in London always decided which new provincial

A Sister Of Mercy shows sympathy for the devil. The Sisters, from Leeds, were just one of the many northern bands to gain hip credibility during the post-punk era of the late Seventies and early Eighties.

outfits were worthy of their patronage, making the occasional trip north – usually to Liverpool – whenever it was agreed that a new band could be given the paper's front-cover endorsement. More often than not, their choices seemed to be random. Critics of their policy could do worse than point to the scores of music press-approved bands 'launched' every year by hopeful record companies, never to be heard of again.

Policing of the provinces by the industry's talent-spotting A&R (Artists and Repertoire) staff was similarly inept. It was virtually impossible for new bands – especially those from unfashionable towns – to get through to the majors, whose inability to monitor what was happening meant that they often signed the wrong bands. All the major post-punk provincial outfits – Echo and the Bunnymen, Orchestral Manoeuvres in the Dark, Gang of Four, Human League and Soft Cell among them – debuted on independent labels and subsequently switched to majors not because the majors discovered them but because their indie mentors needed help. In many ways, the new provincial independent labels were the A&R departments of the London majors.

The Zoo gang
The first decisive events in the story of provincial post-punk were the formation of two vastly important independent labels: Liverpool's Zoo and Manchester's Factory. Both these were crucial in that they showed the nascent independent scene that it was possible to be influential, tasteful and commercially viable on a shoestring budget. Echo and the Bunnymen's 'Pictures On My Wall' (released on Zoo in 1978) and Orchestral Manoeuvres' superbly packaged 'Electricity' (Factory, 1979) had a particularly big impact, both critically and industrially. Labels like Glasgow's Postcard Records, Norwich's Backs and Sheffield's Pax all took their cue from the early product of Zoo and Factory Records.

Simultaneously influential was Edinburgh's Fast Product, on which the Human League made their debut with 'Electronically Yours' in June 1978, and the Gang of Four unveiled their 'radical dance music' via the *Damaged Goods* EP in October 1978. The no-compromise Gang of Four were perhaps lucky to get this break, there being no significant independent label in Yorkshire – or in the whole of the eastern part of the country for that matter at the time. In any event, the band subsequently consolidated their national audience following a deal with EMI, for whom they recorded the early classic 'At Home He's A Tourist' in 1979.

The peak years of regional activity between 1979 and 1981 answered a lot of questions as punk panned out. Hot on the heels of Echo and the Bunnymen, the Teardrop Explodes and Birkenhead's OMD came the second wave of Liverpool bands: Inevitable Records' Wah! and Nightmares in Wax (who became Dead or Alive), later with WEA and Epic Records respectively, and Modern Eon (briefly with the Virgin off-shoot, DinDisc). Sheffield too 'exploded' with bands like Clock DVA, I'm So Hollow, They Must Be Russians and the Comsat Angels; Leeds meantime blew hot and cold with

the Expelaires (who had debuted on Zoo in 1979); Manchester, already oozing 'credibility' through Magazine, Buzzcocks and the Fall, now revealed subtlety via various new Factory bands, notably Durutti Column.

These were key years in other ways too. A particularly important development was the trend towards DIY singles – mostly by bands who could take no more standard rejection slips from the majors. Two Leeds bands that used this route to decisive effect were Soft Cell – soon to star on 1981's *Some Bizarre* compilation – and Girls At Our Best, whose 'Warm Girls' and two follow-ups made them the flavour of many a month. Later, the same city's Sisters of Mercy became past masters of the DIY method, their Merciful Release label enjoying success well into the Eighties.

The simultaneous rise of independent distributors like Pinnacle, Spartan and the Cartel of five provincial independent labels and Rough Trade in London facilitated the DIY approach and continued to democratise the rock scene for small labels. So too did the Alternative Charts, compiled by the Media Research and Information Bureau. A band that appeared in these got noticed by both the industry and the media – and it took ludicrously low sales figures to achieve this. Hull's Red Guitars, for instance, entered the chart in July 1983 having sold 34 copies of their first DIY single 'Good Technology' nationally during the previous week.

As the new decade progressed, however, it was becoming increasingly clear that there were far too many bands – literally thousands of them looking for record deals at any given time – for the music industry to cope with. The huge numbers of bands involved made it impossible for all of them to be auditioned, let alone signed. The situation was such that many promising outfits went to the wall during this period, not because they were not good but because they were not *needed*.

Too much pressure
The industry's various crises (not least its perennial home-taping dilemma) around this time resulted in all the London majors reducing their artist rosters, so that it was becoming even more difficult to get a record deal. Although the resulting frustration drove many a regional-based outfit to call it a day, the more resilient became even more uncompromising – and, because they made no attempt to be commercial, their music benefited in terms of originality.

After many of the major northern towns and cities had yielded promising acts, similar scenes began to develop throughout the country, their success depending to a large extent on attracting the attention of the music press. This trend continued into 1982 when, as a result of the majors' obsession with image and hit singles, the disgusted rock press turned north for protégés with 'integrity': the previously mentioned Southern Death Cult (Bradford), Danse Society (Barnsley) and the Sisters of Mercy (Leeds) were among the newly favoured.

NIGEL BURNHAM

*The northlands explode! Jon King of Leeds'
Gang of Four (opposite top), Pete Burns of
Liverpool's Dead or Alive (opposite below),
Bradford's Southern Death Cult (opposite
bottom), Sheffield's Comsat Angels (right),
and Barnsley's Danse Society (below).
Uncompromising and committed new-wave
acts such as these proved that England's rock
scene of the Eighties did not revolve entirely
around the country's capital.*

ROCK '80

In 1980, the previous year's great hopes – Blondie, the Police and the Pretenders – were joined in the UK charts by such new acts as Dexys Midnight Runners and Adam and the Ants. Adam Ant also brought a new wave of fashion to the fore, with his swashbuckling dress and sophisticated make-up – a style suggested by punk Svengali Malcolm McLaren and soon adopted by the emerging new romantic groups such as Spandau Ballet, Ultravox and Visage. The latter featured fashion leader Steve Strange.

The previous year's Mod revival, without any strong figurehead, began to lose momentum, although the Jam stayed the pace by proving their diversity and talent. 1980 saw another surge of nostalgia with the revival of rockabilly through the Stray Cats, the Polecats and Matchbox. Heavy metal received fresh wind with such new bands as Def Leppard, Iron Maiden and Saxon, America's Van Halen and Canada's Rush, while former members of Deep Purple prospered as key members of Rainbow, Gillan and Whitesnake. Other veterans like Elton John, Paul McCartney and the Rolling Stones continued to churn out hit albums, while in the US Bruce Springsteen and Tom Petty flourished along with Queen, the Eagles, Billy Joel, Christopher Cross and newcomer Rickie Lee Jones.

The UK singles charts were varied and lively in 1980, with the usual smattering of quirky novelty records. Actor Keith Michell (better known as television's Henry VIII) made the Top Ten in February with the double A-sided 'Captain Beaky'/'Wilfred The Weasel', while a bunch of angelic schoolchildren, St Winifred's School Choir, charmed the hearts of the nation at Christmas with 'No One Quite Like Grandma'. On the alternative scene, the new darlings to emerge from the Northern gloom, Joy Division, were shattered by the suicide of their frontman Ian Curtis, while music fans of all ages the world over were shocked by the tragic killing of John Lennon at the end of the year.

January

7 Hugh Cornwell of the Stranglers is found guilty of possessing heroin, cocaine and cannabis. He is sentenced to eight weeks in jail and fined £300.
16 Paul McCartney is put in a Tokyo prison when eight ounces of marijuana is found in his luggage. The Wings tour of Japan is cancelled, but McCartney is released after 10 days.

Above: David Bowie made his stage acting debut in July playing the title role in 'The Elephant Man'. Below: Bow Wow Wow, featuring teenage singer Annabella Lwin, began their bid for pop success in February.

18 The Pretenders' debut LP *Pretenders*, enters the UK charts at Number 1.
26 The Specials' 'Too Much Too Young' gives them their first UK Number 1 single.

February

8 David Bowie is divorced from Angie and wins custody of their son, Zowie.
19 AC/DC singer Bon Scott is found dead in a car in London, having choked on his own vomit after a night of heavy drinking.

22 Malcolm McLaren sacks Adam from the Ants who, fronted by schoolgirl Annabella Lwin, become Bow Wow Wow.

March

3 At Sotheby's, the London auction house, a paper napkin signed by Elvis Presley fetches £500 and a banknote signed by the Beatles goes for £220.
15 The Clash film *Rude Boy* opens at the Prince Charles Theatre, London.
21 The Jam's 'Going Underground' enters the UK singles chart at Number 1.
25 The Police play in Bombay – the first rock band to appear in India since Hawkwind 10 years previously.

April

19 Beggar's Banquet release the first video of any British artist to be available to the public. Selling at £19.99, it covers 45 minutes of a Gary Numan concert at London's Hammersmith Odeon the previous year.
22 Dexys Midnight Runners top the UK singles charts with only their second single, 'Geno'.
26 Blondie's single 'Call Me' is Number 1 on both sides of the Atlantic.

May

1 The first issue of the *Face*, a new monthly rock magazine, is published in Britain.
2 Pink Floyd's single 'Another Brick In The Wall Part Two' is banned by the South African authorities because black schoolchildren had adopted the song as a protest against their second-rate education system.
17 Joy Division's singer Ian Curtis hangs himself shortly after the band complete their second album *Closer*.
21 Joe Strummer of the Clash is arrested by German police for smashing a guitar

The blueprint for the independent music labels that were to foster the boom in Scottish music was Zoom Records in Edinburgh. The label was formed by Bruce Findlay, who had run the successful Bruce's chain of record stores with his brother until the mid-Seventies price-cutting war put them out of business. Zoom released their first record, 'For Adults Only'/'Robot Love' by the Valves, in September 1977 and rapidly became a clearing house for young Scots hopefuls: Midge Ure, later of the Rich Kids and Ultravox, was an early Zoom act, recording for the label with his band Slik under the pseudonym PVC2. The label also passed on the Associates' early demos – including a cover of Bowie's 'Boys Keep Swinging', eventually released on MCA – before striking it lucky with Simple Minds.

Originally a punk band from Glasgow called Johnny and the Self Abusers, Simple Minds turned out to be the commercial giants of the Scottish boom. Their three albums for Zoom/Arista sold in substantial quantities before the band signed to Virgin and had hit albums with *Sons And Fascination/Sister Feelings Call* (1981), *New Gold Dream* (1982) and *Sparkle In The Rain* (1984).

Round the Horne

Whereas Bruce Findlay could be seen as a father figure to the fledgling Scots bands he signed, Postcard Records' Alan Horne was in the same age group as his early signings Orange Juice, Josef K and Aztec Camera. Postcard's early output was well received – ecstatically in some quarters – and for a while, in 1980 and 1981, the names Postcard and Alan Horne were on everybody's lips. Orange Juice earned much of the early praise with a fine succession of early singles: 'Falling And Laughing', 'Blueboy', 'Simply Thrilled Honey' (all 1980) and 'Poor Old Soul' (1981). In addition to his songwriting abilities, lead singer and guitarist Edwyn Collins was a natural showman, and the music press took him to their hearts.

Aztec Camera shared Orange Juice's gift for gentle, acoustic arrangements which subtly evoked a variety of subdued emotions. After signing to Postcard in 1980, they released two highly acclaimed singles, 'Just Like Gold' and 'Mattress Of Wire' and went through a number of personnel changes, although the nucleus of the group remained singer, songwriter and guitarist Roddy Frame and bassist Campbell Owens. In 1982, they signed to Rough Trade, and recorded their debut album, *High Land, Hard Rain*, before moving to WEA Records to enjoy a Top Twenty hit single, 'Oblivious', in 1983.

Stablemates Josef K were equally promising. Although their early output was overshadowed by that of Orange Juice, 'Radio Drill Time' and 'It's Kinda Funny' (both 1980) were excellent singles. Disagreements between the band's two frontmen, Paul Haig and guitarist Malcolm Ross, over recording techniques led to the

Orange Juice

Much of Orange Juice's early charm lay in their naivety and coyness which, although endearing to some, was insufferable to others. Their early Postcard singles, 'Blueboy', 'Falling And Laughing' (both 1980) and 'Poor Old Soul' (1981) had a certain magic, but by the time they signed to Polydor and released their first LP, *You Can't Hide Your Love Forever* (1982), the appeal of singer Edwyn Collins' fey looks and wistful songs was wearing thin. Enough fans bought the album, however, to keep it in the charts for some six weeks, peaking at Number 21. Two minor hit singles sprang from the album, guitarist James Kirk's 'Felicity' and a ragged attempt at a cover of the Al Green classic 'L.O.V.E.'

Collins then reformed the band completely; out went Kirk and drummer Steven Daly, to be replaced by Malcolm Ross – from former Postcard stable-

Above: Orange Juice singer Edwyn Collins, a constant factor in the group's changing line-up.

mates Josef K – and Zeke Manyika respectively, leaving only Collins and bassist Davie McClymont from the previous line-up. This had the effect of toughening up the band and cutting away the cuteness, while retaining the more durable elements of their early sound. Their image changed accordingly: Edwyn abandoned his furry hats, cuddly fringe and boyish shorts for natty suits and a spruce haircut.

A second album, *Rip It Up*, was released at the end of 1982 and the title track became the band's biggest hit single, reaching Number 8 in the UK charts the following spring. David and Malcolm then left, and the band survived until the autumn of 1984.

BERT MUIRHEAD

group's break-up. Ross later joined Orange Juice, while Haig pursued a solo career. An album, *The Only Fun In Town* (1981), was released after the group's demise.

By mid-1981, Postcard Records was at its peak, and so was the Scottish music scene in general. A number of good Scottish contributors to the weekly music press ensured that the scene received regular coverage, while Glasgow – which for years had had very few good music venues – suddenly produced a number of new nightclubs and discos. A whole crop of exciting new bands sprang up: the Fire Engines, with their gritty, punky instrumentals, the more traditional TV21, the poppy Delmontes, the President's Men, the Laughing Apple, APB, Leisure Process, the Bluebells, Hey Elastica!, Boots For Dancing, Bourgie Bourgie, the Jazzateers and a host of others.

The north of Scotland also produced its own music scene. Aberdeen was the home of Oily Records, which enjoyed some early success with singles by the President's Men, the Squibs and the Tools, before things really took off with the success of local band APB. Their second single, 'I'd Like To Shoot You Down' (1981) found its way to an FM station in Philadelphia, and from there to the New York clubs. A promotions firm called Rockpool circulated the single to 200 clubs, radio stations and DJs. They were soon playing on the same bill as soul star James Brown.

Simple Minds

GLASGOW'S SIMPLE MINDS – singer Jim Kerr, guitarist Charlie Burchill, drummer Brian McGee, keyboard player Michael McNeill and bassist Derek Forbes – originally signed to Zoom Records, but a distribution deal was soon arranged through Arista. Their first three LPs – *Life In A Day, Real To Real Cacophony* (both 1979) and *Empires And Dance* (1980) – were a strange mixture of influences,

Above: Simple Minds keep feeling fascination. Left: Singer Jim Kerr puts his trousers to the test.

from Roxy Music to Sixties psychedelia, and ranged from the very serious to the eminently danceable.

It was the third of these that consolidated their reputation and contained the best song of their early days, 'I Travel'. After a prestigious European tour with Peter Gabriel in 1980, they signed to Virgin Records and recorded their strongest albums to date, *Sons And Fascination* and *Sister Feelings Call* (initially issued together as a double-pack but later sold separately), and reached the Number 11 position in the album chart.

The band were now rapidly establishing themselves, and some excellent promotional videos kept up the momentum during the band's extensive tours. In 1982, their album *New Gold Dream* soared to Number 3 in the UK and also did well in the US. Two Top Twenty singles followed, 'Promised You A Miracle' and 'Glittering Prize'. A UK Top Ten single, 'Waterfront', and another series of tours in 1983, established the career that is more significantly explored in Volume 20.

BERT MUIRHEAD

Dundee cakewalk

Dundee was the home of the Associates, whose rise to success was as sudden as their fall from it. The Associates were basically the duo of Alan Rankine and vocalist Billie Mackenzie, although they worked with other musicians like former Cure bassist Michael Dempsey and drummer John Murphy. Their debut album, *The Affectionate Punch* (1980), wedded intense, Bowie-influenced soul vocals with abrasive, 'experimental' sounds, and was released on Fiction Records to extravagant critical praise in 1980. After a spell on Situation 2 Records, they signed to WEA and enjoyed a series of UK hit singles – 'Party Fears Two' (Number 9), 'Club Country' (Number 13) and '18 Carat Love Affair'/'Love Hangover' (Number 21) – in 1982. Their 1982 LP, *Sulk*, also

Aztec Camera (above) started life on Postcard Records before going on to have a Top Twenty hit with 'Oblivious' in 1983.

made the UK album chart Top Ten, but the Associates could not live up to the intense commercial expectations their success brought about, and split early in 1983.

Rankine and Mackenzie got together again a couple of years later, however. A band called the Shakin' Pyramids from Glasgow did much to pioneer the rockabilly revival, only to be overshadowed by the Stray Cats, while TV21, whose debut album *The Thin Red Line* (1981) was widely praised, split up after supporting the Rolling Stones on the Scottish dates of their 1982 tour.

But if the Scottish boom had given some bands unrealistic hopes, it also put the country on the map. The success of Simple Minds, Orange Juice and Big Country ensured a bright future for Scottish music.   BERT MUIRHEAD

Skids

THE SKIDS were one of the first of the Scottish bands to make a breakthrough at the end of the Seventies. Their early single, 'Reasons', released on No Bad Records of Dunfermline in 1978, regular appearances in the pages of the punk fanzines and the patronage of John Peel led to a contract with Virgin Records. Lead singer Richard Jobson became the darling of the music press and he was keen to live up to his media image as a literary dilettante.

Together with guitarist Stuart Adamson, Jobson formed a songwriting team that produced 10 hit singles in just over two years. Their first LP, the raw and punky *Scared To Dance*, spent 10 weeks in the album charts early in 1979, while the single from it, 'Into The Valley', reached Number 10. Their second LP, *Days In Europa* (1979), contained the hit singles 'Charade' and 'Working For The Yankee Dollar'.

However, Jobson's growing artistic pretentions – which found their way onto the Skids' third album *The Absolute Game* (1980) – were alienating Stuart Adamson, who quit soon after the LP's release. Jobson carried on with bassist Russell Webb, recording a final album, *Joy* (1981), which explored Celtic folksong. He then retired from the music scene to pursue his interests in acting and poetry. He returned to rock singing in 1983 with a new band, the Armoury Show, but this new project was overshadowed by his former sidekick Stuart Adamson, who had refined the basic Skids sound with his group, Big Country, and was storming the charts on both sides of the Atlantic.   BERT MUIRHEAD

Below: Jobson (centre) with future Big Country guitarist Stuart Adamson (right).

ECHO and the BUNNYMEN

The pride of the Liverpool scene

IF LONDON SEEMED to be the focal point of attention and activity in rock music during 1976 and 1977 as punk rose to its peak of excitement, by the beginning of 1978, the emphasis was beginning to shift away from the capital. For a few years at least, the most intriguing musical developments would occur elsewhere in the UK.

The age of innocence
In Liverpool, punk had had its day and a number of the city's would-be musicians and legendary heroes – Pete Wylie, Julian Cope and Ian 'Mac' McCulloch among them – were seeking to become involved in music that was richer, stranger and more adventurous. These three individuals had briefly formed a group called the Crucial Three before ego-clashes led to a split, with Wylie and Cope respectively drifting off to form Wah! Heat and the Teardrop Explodes.

Ian McCulloch was every bit as determined to become a rock legend as his former partners; he started looking around for kindred spirits who shared his passion for the sounds and styles of David Bowie and the Velvet Underground. After the failure of a further venture, A Shallow Madness, he met bassist Les Pattison and guitarist Will Sergeant at Eric's in Liverpool and Echo and the Bunnymen began to take shape. Gigging in their home town in the autumn of 1978, using a drum machine (which became known as 'Echo'), they soon attracted the interest of entrepreneurs Bill Drummond and Dave Balfe, who were looking for bands to sign to their independent Zoo label.

From the very start the Bunnymen were determined to succeed. Their comparative inexperience as musicians and performers helped them avoid the clichés of most rock groups, while their unswerving belief in

themselves soon won them a considerable following. The androgynously pretty McCulloch (rhythm guitar and lead vocals) proved to be a truly charismatic frontman; his obscure but bleakly humorous lyrics helped define the band's intriguing, brooding sound, which was reminiscent of the Doors and Television in its spare clarity. Among a crop of independent singles released in March 1979, Echo and the Bunnymen's 'Pictures On My Wall' (featuring keyboards by David Balfe) had the edge, encouraging critics to link their name with Manchester's Joy Division as two of the bands most likely to lead rock music into exciting new areas.

Tigers in the smoke

As their reputation spread, Pete De Freitas joined on drums to instil the power that the drum machine had lacked. 'Rescue', their second single (released in April 1980) established them as *the* emerging cult band, while their debut LP, the critically acclaimed *Crocodiles* (1980), demonstrated their great potential. As Mac was to boast at the end of that year, which was to see the album make Number 17 in the UK charts: 'It feels like there's hundreds of bands in Liverpool, but we're about the only one I can think of as being a potentially *great* band.'

During the course of regular touring over the next 12 months, they entered their controversial 'camouflage' phase. In an attempt to intensify their already considerable live impact, they created a steamy jungle atmosphere, with lashings of dry ice and rolls of camouflage netting, that was reminiscent of the Francis Ford Coppola film *Apocalypse Now* (1979). This uncharacteristic extravagance brought them their first taste of harsh criticism in the rock press; a subsequent single, 'The Puppet' (released in the winter of 1980), drew only lukewarm praise.

The band's optimism remained undimmed by these minor setbacks, however: in the following year they took part in a video film, *Shine So Hard*, which contained footage of the group playing live at the Pavilion Gardens, Buxton. An EP, also entitled *Shine So Hard*, was released in May and took them into the UK Top Thirty for the first time.

Their next LP, *Heaven Up Here* (1981), finally established them as a major force, being voted Album of the Year by readers of *New Musical Express* and making Number 10 in the charts. Their manager Bill Drummond summed up the mood and mythical qualities of their songs at this time when he wrote in the *Face*: 'They represent cold, dampness, darkness. Echo is, in my crazy daydream, a ghostly God – and the Bunnymen are his followers.'

The next year, however, proved to be a particularly difficult one for the group, despite chart success with 'The Back Of Love' (a Number 19 hit). With this single, perhaps the nearest the Bunnymen had come to a pure pop sound, their appeal stretched to the teenage pin-up market for

Opposite: Echo and the Bunnymen in 'moody' pose; clockwise from left Ian McCulloch, Will Sergeant, Pete De Freitas and Les Pattison. Above: 'Mac' shows off his haircut. Below: Real live Bunnies.

the first time. This sudden development seemed to confuse the band; although their live performances constantly gained in authority, they appeared to be having trouble writing new songs. *Heaven Up Here*'s successor, *Porcupine*, took 18 months to appear, being released in 1983.

Although the single taken from it, 'The Cutter' (a Number 8 hit) showed them at their most coherent, uncluttered and uplifting, the remainder of the LP failed to equal the power of its predecessor.

The new year brought a taste of startling new developments with the single 'The Killing Moon'. This powerful song featured the melodramatic string arrangements that were to characterise the Bunnymen's fourth album, *Ocean Rain*. Released in May 1984, the album produced two more

hit singles, 'Silver' and 'Seven Seas'. The latter was also released on a 12 inch EP along with acoustic versions of earlier Bunnymen songs and of the Beatles' 'All You Need Is Love'.

More than a year was to pass, however, before their next single, 'Bring On The Dancing Horses', and a compilation LP, *Songs To Learn And Sing*, confirmed Echo and the Bunnymen as one of those few bands in the Eighties making rock music of rare, consuming rapture and lyrical depth. The group split in November 1988 after that year's eponymous LP, Ian McCulloch intent on a solo career, with the other three's future uncertain.   JONH WILDE

**Echo and the Bunnyman
Recommended Listening**

Heaven Up Here (Korova KOW 58 320) (Includes: The Disease, Heaven Up Here, Turquoise Dogs, Show Of Strength, It Was A Pleasure, No Dark Things); *Porcupine* (Korova KODE 6) (Includes: The Cutter, Porcupine, Higher Hell, Gods Will Be Gods, Heads Will Roll, Back Of Love).

Eric's AND AFTER

The club that harboured a new Mersey beat

IN 1964, LIVERPOOL had been the pop music capital of the world. The Beatles had conquered America and a host of other Merseybeat acts were attempting to emulate the feats of the Fab Four. But when the Mersey boom burned out later in the decade, Liverpool was left with no identifiable rock scene of its own. At the end of the Seventies, however, the city drew breath and prepared itself to hit the country again with a new breed of home-grown music.

Although the musical outlooks of Sixties Merseybeat and the Seventies new wave were very different, they had two things in common: both scenes centred around, and grew out of, one specific club – the Cavern in the case of Merseybeat, Eric's in the Seventies – and both scenes were highly incestuous in nature, with groups trading ideas and swapping personnel quite regularly.

The new sound of Liverpool can be traced back to January 1974 when a collection of Liverpool art-school students formed a band called Deaf School. Unlike any Liverpudlian group before, Deaf School were a camp, theatrical, arty band whose music was criticised as being over-derivative of Roxy Music. Despite three strong albums for Warner Brothers, Deaf School's following remained largely local and in 1978 they disbanded.

Crucial relations

Among Deaf School's musicians, now let loose on a revitalised music scene, had been Clive Langer (later to produce Liverpool's own the Teardrop Explodes and the Yachts as well as Madness), Bette Bright (who went on to enjoy a reasonably successful solo career), Steve Lindsey (later to join Big in Japan and then form the Planets) and Steve Allen (who in December 1978 teamed up with ex-Big in Japan guitarist Ian Broudie to form the London-based Original Mirrors).

Deaf School fans were also to play crucial roles in the development of Liverpool's new age. Three of the group's most devoted followers had been David Balfe (who was to play with Radio Blank, Dalek I Love You, Big in Japan, Lori and the Chameleons and the Teardrop Explodes), Pete Wylie (who would form Wah! Heat) and Ian McCulloch (who would form Echo and the Bunnymen). They would religiously turn up at Deaf School gigs and afterwards congregate in the trendy Arts Theatre café. Trendy, that is, until the opening of Eric's in 1976.

Situated symbolically near the rubble that had been the Cavern, Eric's was just as dingy. Under the managerial auspices of ex-public relations man Roger Eagle, the club remained the showplace for any punk band that would play there until its enforced closure in March 1980. Often bands were booked for the sheer idiocy of their name and any group who claimed to be Liverpudlian would be guaranteed a stage, however bad they were.

On 5 May 1977 the Clash played Eric's; in the audience were McCulloch, Wylie and Julian Cope who, brought together by the sheer physical compression of the place, decided that they too must form a band. The prophetically-named Crucial Three never played live and split up after only a month, McCulloch's love for melodic tunes clashing with Cope's devotion to the avant-garde American group Pere Ubu. Nevertheless, the seeds had been sown of a desire to make music and of a creative rivalry that was to dominate their respective careers.

The art of bluff

At the same Clash gig, 23-year-old ex-theatre manager Bill Drummond had also been inspired to form a band and, with various friends, put together Big in Japan, a band that was to become the missing link between the theatrics of Deaf School and the amateurism of punk. They played trashy pop, went through five line-ups and came up for many a potential record deal. However, in August 1978 they played their final gig at Eric's and Drummond decided to form an independent record label with fellow group member David Balfe.

While Stiff and Rough Trade undermined the stranglehold of the big companies in the South, the only northern indie label of note was Factory in Manchester. But now, with financial support from the Merseyside Visual Communications Unit, the Zoo label swung into action with a farewell Big in Japan EP, *From Y To Z And Never Again*.

Following the swift demise of the Crucial Three, meanwhile, Cope, McCulloch and Pete Wylie had formed, disbanded and re-formed groups, together and separately, which were, as often as not, just a ridiculous name with no words or music. It was not until late 1978, when Cope and McCulloch played debut gigs at Eric's with their new bands, the Teardrop Explodes and Echo and the Bunnymen, that they showed signs of forging careers in music. Both groups were swiftly signed up by Zoo, who released their first singles early in 1979.

Pete Wylie was slower to make his vinyl debut. He formed his own Wah! Heat in 1979 and the group's first single, 'Better Scream'/'Joe', emerged the following February on the independent Inevitable label. Dropping the Heat from their name, Wah! formed their own Eternal label which was distributed by WEA. Their debut album, *Nah Poo – The Art Of Bluff*

Above left: The Teardrop Explodes on stage shortly before their demise in 1982. Top right: Pete Wylie of Wah! adjusts his cap for the camera. Above right: The crowds gather outside Eric's, the club where the new sound of Liverpool was born. Right: Julian Cope ponders.

brought the Teardrop Explodes to a halt in 1982. Cope's solo LPs *World Shut Your Mouth* (1984), *Fried* (1984), *St Julian* (1986) and *My Nation Underground* (1988) established him as a cult figure without bringing great success.

The triple echo

To Cope's probable dismay, it was his arch-rival Ian McCulloch's Echo and the Bunnymen who were to prove the most successful of all the new Liverpudlian acts, with consistently high album sales and a large and devoted following. When their second album, *Heaven Up Here*, was voted Album of the Year in the 1981 *New Musical Express* reader's poll, the Bunnymen had come a long way from playing shambolic gigs with a drum machine at Eric's.

In many ways, to talk of a 'Liverpool sound' is misleading, for the new scene encompassed such a wide range of musical ideas – from the power pop of the Planets, through the primal scream antics of Pink Military (fronted by former Big in Japan *chanteuse* Jayne Casey) to the minimalist electro-rock of Dalek I Love You, to cite just three examples. Although Merseyside's new wave had nothing like the impact of Merseybeat, it was an exciting, vibrant movement which guaranteed that Liverpool would be remembered as a musical city for the Eighties as it had been for the Sixties.   SALLY PAYNE

(1981) was a commercial disaster, however, and it was not until 1983 that they began to realise their potential with 'The Story Of The Blues', an epic, Phil Spector-inspired number which reached Number 3 in the singles charts in January.

Above: Deaf School proved to be a strong influence on Liverpool's new bands. Below: Electro-rockers Dalek I Love You.

Treason in the playroom

Meanwhile, the Teardrop Explodes, named after a line in a Marvel comic strip, had gone through a succession of line-ups under the headstrong domination of Julian Cope. Contrary to the stark, depressed coldness of many of their contemporaries, the Teardrop Explodes played pop music with melodies – and, despite Cope's uncompromising attitude to the rock business, the band was signed by Mercury in the summer of 1980. In October, *Kilimanjaro*, a fine collection of intriguing songs that revealed Julian Cope's growing interest in Sixties psychedelia, reached Number 24 in the album charts and the following February the group scored a Number 6 hit with 'Reward', a wonderfully theatrical number based around a strong vocal melody, melodramatic horns and distinctive keyboards.

Soon the Teardrop Explodes were appearing on BBC-TV's 'Top Of The Pops', identified as the band in leather flying jackets and acclaimed as the forerunners of a Liverpool explosion. Further hit singles followed with 'Treason (It's Just A Story)' (Number 18) and the Sixties pop-tinged 'Passionate Friend' (Number 25), while a second album, *Wilder* (1981), confirmed Cope's psychedelic obsessions, both lyrically and musically, and reached Number 29. However, squabbles within the group had led to numerous personnel changes, and Cope's egotistical leadership finally

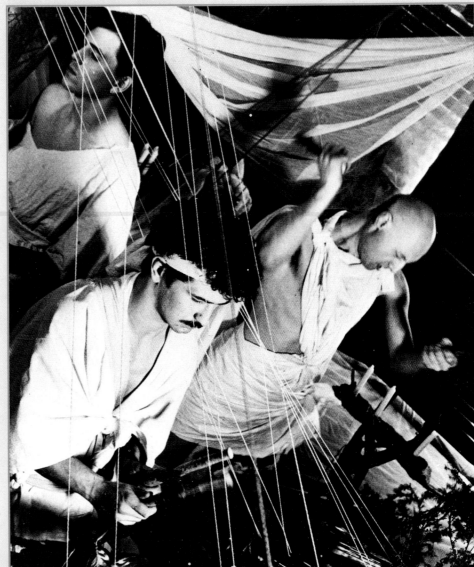

INDEX

U.S. HIT SINGLES

1986

JANUARY

4   SAY YOU, SAY ME   *Lionel Richie*
11 SAY YOU, SAY ME   *Lionel Richie*
18 THAT'S WHAT FRIENDS ARE FOR
    Dionne Warwick and Friends
25 THAT'S WHAT FRIENDS ARE FOR
    Dionne Warwick and Friends

FEBRUARY

1   THAT'S WHAT FRIENDS ARE FOR
    Dionne Warwick and Friends
8   THAT'S WHAT FRIENDS ARE FOR
    Dionne Warwick and Friends
15 HOW WILL I KNOW   *Whitney Houston*
22 HOW WILL I KNOW   *Whitney Houston*

MARCH

1   KYRIE   *Mr Mister*
8   KYRIE   *Mr Mister*
15 SARA   *Starship*
22 THESE DREAMS   *Heart*
29 ROCK ME AMADEUS   *Falco*

APRIL

5   ROCK ME AMADEUS   *Falco*
12 ROCK ME AMADEUS   *Falco*
19 KISS   *Prince*
26 KISS   *Prince*

MAY

3   ADDICTED TO LOVE   *Robert Palmer*
10 WEST END GIRLS   *Pet Shop Boys*
17 THE GREATEST LOVE OF ALL   *Whitney Houston*
24 THE GREATEST LOVE OF ALL   *Whitney Houston*
31 THE GREATEST LOVE OF ALL   *Whitney Houston*

JUNE

7   LIVE TO TELL   *Madonna*
14 ON MY OWN   *Patti LaBelle and Michael McDonald*
21 ON MY OWN   *Patti LaBelle and Michael McDonald*
28 ON MY OWN   *Patti LaBelle and Michael McDonald*

JULY

5   THERE'LL BE SAD SONGS   *Billy Ocean*
12 HOLDING BACK THE YEARS   *Simply Red*
19 INVISIBLE TOUCH   *Genesis*
26 SLEDGEHAMMER   *Peter Gabriel*

AUGUST

2   GLORY OF LOVE   *Peter Cetera*
9   GLORY OF LOVE   *Peter Cetera*
16 PAPA DON'T PREACH   *Madonna*
23 PAPA DON'T PREACH   *Madonna*
30 HIGHER LOVE   *Steve Winwood*

SEPTEMBER

6   VENUS   *Bananarama*
13 TAKE MY BREATH AWAY   *Berlin*
20 STUCK WITH YOU   *Huey Lewis and the News*
27 STUCK WITH YOU   *Huey Lewis and the News*

OCTOBER

4   STUCK WITH YOU   *Huey Lewis and the News*
11 WHEN I THINK OF YOU   *Janet Jackson*
18 WHEN I THINK OF YOU   *Janet Jackson*
25 TRUE COLOURS   *Cyndi Lauper*

NOVEMBER

1   TRUE COLOURS   *Cyndi Lauper*
8   AMANDA   *Boston*
15 AMANDA   *Boston*
22 HUMAN   *Human League*
29 YOU GIVE LOVE A BAD NAME   *Bon Jovi*

DECEMBER

6   THE NEXT TIME I FALL   *Peter Cetera and Amy Grant*
13 THE WAY IT IS   *Bruce Hornsby and the Range*
20 WALK LIKE AN EGYPTIAN   *Bangles*
27 WALK LIKE AN EGYPTIAN   *Bangles*

1987

JANUARY

3 WALK LIKE AN EGYPTIAN *Bangles*
10 WALK LIKE AN EGYPTIAN *Bangles*
17 SHAKE YOU DOWN *Gregory Abbott*
24 AT THIS MOMENT *Billy Vera & The Beaters*
31 AT THIS MOMENT *Billy Vera & The Beaters*

FEBRUARY

7 OPEN YOUR HEART *Madonna*
14 LIVIN' ON A PRAYER *Bon Jovi*
21 LIVIN' ON A PRAYER *Bon Jovi*
28 LIVIN' ON A PRAYER *Bon Jovi*

MARCH

7 LIVIN' ON A PRAYER *Bon Jovi*
14 JACOB'S LADDER *Huey Lewis and The News*
21 LEAN ON ME *Club Nouveau*
28 LEAN ON ME *Club Nouveau*

APRIL

4 NOTHING'S GONNA STOP US NOW *Starship*
11 NOTHING'S GONNA STOP US NOW *Starship*
18 I KNEW YOU WERE WAITING
    Aretha Franklin/George Michael
25 I KNEW YOU WERE WAITING
    Aretha Franklin/George Michael

MAY

2 (I JUST) DIED IN YOUR ARMS *Cutting Crew*
9 (I JUST) DIED IN YOUR ARMS *Cutting Crew*
16 WITH OR WITHOUT YOU *U2*
23 WITH OR WITHOUT YOU *U2*
30 WITH OR WITHOUT YOU *U2*

JUNE

6 YOU KEEP ME HANGIN' ON *Kim Wilde*
13 ALWAYS *Atlantic Starr*
20 HEAD TO TOE *Lisa Lisa/Cult Jam*
27 I WANNA DANCE WITH SOMEBODY *Whitney Houston*

JULY

6 I WANNA DANCE WITH SOMEBODY *Whitney Houston*
11 ALONE *Heart*
18 ALONE *Heart*
25 ALONE *Heart*

AUGUST

1 SHAKEDOWN *Bob Seger*
8 I STILL HAVEN'T FOUND WHAT I'M LOOKING FOR *U2*
15 I STILL HAVEN'T FOUND WHAT I'M LOOKING FOR *U2*
22 WHO'S THAT GIRL *Madonna*
29 LA BAMBA *Los Lobos*

SEPTEMBER

5 LA BAMBA *Los Lobos*
12 LA BAMBA *Los Lobos*
19 I JUST CAN'T STOP LOVING YOU *Michael Jackson*
26 DIDN'T WE ALMOST HAVE IT ALL *Whitney Houston*

OCTOBER

3 DIDN'T WE ALMOST HAVE IT ALL *Whitney Houston*
10 HERE I GO AGAIN *Whitesnake*
17 LOST IN EMOTION *Lisa Lisa/Cult Jam*
24 BAD *Michael Jackson*
31 BAD *Michael Jackson*

NOVEMBER

7 I THINK WE'RE ALONE NOW *Tiffany*
14 I THINK WE'RE ALONE NOW *Tiffany*
21 MONY MONY *Billy Idol*
28 (I'VE HAD) THE TIME OF MY LIFE
    Bill Medley/Jennifer Warnes

DECEMBER

5 HEAVEN IS A PLACE ON EARTH *Belinda Carlisle*
12 FAITH *George Michael*
19 FAITH *George Michael*
26 FAITH *George Michael*

U.K. HIT SINGLES

1986

JANUARY

- **4** MERRY CHRISTMAS EVERYONE *Shakin' Stevens*
- **11** WEST END GIRLS *Pet Shop Boys*
- **18** WEST END GIRLS *Pet Shop Boys*
- **25** THE SUN ALWAYS SHINES ON TV *A-Ha*

FEBRUARY

- **1** THE SUN ALWAYS SHINES ON TV *A-Ha*
- **8** WHEN THE GOING GETS TOUGH, THE TOUGH GET GOING *Billy Ocean*
- **15** WHEN THE GOING GETS TOUGH, THE TOUGH GET GOING *Billy Ocean*
- **22** WHEN THE GOING GETS TOUGH, THE TOUGH GET GOING *Billy Ocean*

MARCH

- **1** WHEN THE GOING GETS TOUGH, THE TOUGH GET GOING *Billy Ocean*
- **8** CHAIN REACTION *Diana Ross*
- **15** CHAIN REACTION *Diana Ross*
- **22** CHAIN REACTION *Diana Ross*
- **29** LIVING DOLL *Cliff Richard and the Young Ones*

APRIL

- **5** LIVING DOLL *Cliff Richard and the Young Ones*
- **12** LIVING DOLL *Cliff Richard and the Young Ones*
- **19** A DIFFERENT CORNER *George Michael*
- **26** A DIFFERENT CORNER *George Michael*

MAY

- **3** A DIFFERENT CORNER *George Michael*
- **10** ROCK ME AMADEUS *Falco*
- **17** THE CHICKEN SONG *Spitting Image*
- **24** THE CHICKEN SONG *Spitting Image*
- **31** THE CHICKEN SONG *Spitting Image*

JUNE

- **7** SPIRIT IN THE SKY *Doctor and the Medics*
- **14** SPIRIT IN THE SKY *Doctor and the Medics*
- **21** SPIRIT IN THE SKY *Doctor and the Medics*
- **28** THE EDGE OF HEAVEN *Wham!*

JULY

- **5** THE EDGE OF HEAVEN *Wham!*
- **12** PAPA DON'T PREACH *Madonna*
- **19** PAPA DON'T PREACH *Madonna*
- **26** PAPA DON'T PREACH *Madonna*

AUGUST

- **2** THE LADY IN RED *Chris de Burgh*
- **9** THE LADY IN RED *Chris de Burgh*
- **16** THE LADY IN RED *Chris de Burgh*
- **23** I WANT TO WAKE UP WITH YOU *Boris Gardiner*
- **30** I WANT TO WAKE UP WITH YOU *Boris Gardiner*

SEPTEMBER

- **6** I WANT TO WAKE UP WITH YOU *Boris Gardiner*
- **13** DON'T LEAVE ME THIS WAY *Communards*
- **20** DON'T LEAVE ME THIS WAY *Communards*
- **27** DON'T LEAVE ME THIS WAY *Communards*

OCTOBER

- **4** DON'T LEAVE ME THIS WAY *Communards*
- **11** TRUE BLUE *Madonna*
- **18** EVERY LOSER WINS *Nick Berry*
- **25** EVERY LOSER WINS *Nick Berry*

NOVEMBER

- **1** EVERY LOSER WINS *Nick Berry*
- **8** TAKE MY BREATH AWAY *Berlin*
- **15** TAKE MY BREATH AWAY *Berlin*
- **22** TAKE MY BREATH AWAY *Berlin*
- **29** TAKE MY BREATH AWAY *Berlin*

DECEMBER

- **6** THE FINAL COUNTDOWN *Europe*
- **13** THE FINAL COUNTDOWN *Europe*
- **20** CARAVAN OF LOVE *Housemartins*
- **27** REET PETITE *Jackie Wilson*

1987

JANUARY

3 REET PETITE *Jackie Wilson*
10 REET PETITE *Jackie Wilson*
17 REET PETITE *Jackie Wilson*
24 JACK YOUR BODY *Steve 'Silk' Hurley*
31 JACK YOUR BODY *Steve 'Silk' Hurley*

FEBRUARY

7 I KNEW YOU WERE WAITING
   Aretha Franklin & George Michael
14 I KNEW YOU WERE WAITING
   Aretha Franklin & George Michael
21 STAND BY ME *Ben E King*
28 STAND BY ME *Ben E King*

MARCH

7 STAND BY ME *Ben E King*
14 EVERYTHING I OWN *Boy George*
21 EVERYTHING I OWN *Boy George*
28 RESPECTABLE *Mel & Kim*

APRIL

4 LET IT BE *Ferry Aid*
11 LET IT BE *Ferry Aid*
18 LET IT BE *Ferry Aid*
25 LA ISLA BONITA *Madonna*

MAY

2 LA ISLA BONITA *Madonna*
9 NOTHING'S GONNA STOP US NOW *Starship*
16 NOTHING'S GONNA STOP US NOW *Starship*
23 NOTHING'S GONNA STOP US NOW *Starship*
30 NOTHING'S GONNA STOP US NOW *Starship*

JUNE

6 I WANNA DANCE WITH SOMEBODY *Whitney Houston*
13 I WANNA DANCE WITH SOMEBODY *Whitney Houston*
20 STAR TREKKIN' *The Firm*
27 STAR TREKKIN' *The Firm*

JULY

4 IT'S A SIN *Pet Shop Boys*
11 IT'S A SIN *Pet Shop Boys*
18 IT'S A SIN *Pet Shop Boys*
25 WHO'S THAT GIRL *Madonna*

AUGUST

1 LA BAMBA *Los Lobos*
8 LA BAMBA *Los Lobos*
15 I JUST CAN'T STOP LOVING YOU
   Michael Jackson/ Siedah Garrett
22 I JUST CAN'T STOP LOVING YOU
   Michael Jackson/ Siedah Garrett
29 NEVER GONNA GIVE YOU UP *Rick Astley*

SEPTEMBER

5 NEVER GONNA GIVE YOU UP *Rick Astley*
12 NEVER GONNA GIVE YOU UP *Rick Astley*
19 NEVER GONNA GIVE YOU UP *Rick Astley*
26 NEVER GONNA GIVE YOU UP *Rick Astley*

OCTOBER

3 PUMP UP THE VOLUME *M/A/R/R/S*
10 PUMP UP THE VOLUME *M/A/R/R/S*
17 YOU WIN AGAIN *Bee Gees*
24 YOU WIN AGAIN *Bee Gees*
31 YOU WIN AGAIN *Bee Gees*

NOVEMBER

7 YOU WIN AGAIN *Bee Gees*
14 CHINA IN YOUR HAND *T'Pau*
21 CHINA IN YOUR HAND *T'Pau*
28 CHINA IN YOUR HAND *T'Pau*

DECEMBER

5 CHINA IN YOUR HAND *T'Pau*
12 CHINA IN YOUR HAND *T'Pau*
19 ALWAYS ON MY MIND *Pet Shop Boys*
26 ALWAYS ON MY MIND *Pet Shop Boys*